AN INTRODUCTION

TO

THE AFRICA CENTERED PERSPECTIVE OF HISTORY

by

C. Tsehloane Keto

U.S. Library of Congress Cataloging in Publication Data
Dr. C. Tsehloane Keto

An Introduction To The African-Centered Perspective Of History

Library Of Congress Catalogue Card Number 93-86120

No part of this publication may be reproduced, stored in a retrieval system, or transmitted in any form or by any means, electronic, mechanical photocopying, recording or otherwise, with the prior written permission of the copyright owner and/or the publishers.

Distributed in the USA by
Frontline Distribution International, Inc.
751 East 75th Street
Chicago, IL 60619
Fax (312) 651-9850

All Rights Reserved.
© 1994 Research Associates School Times Publications
U.K office and distributors: Karnak House
300 Westbourne Park Road
London W11, 1EH
England

An Introduction To The African-Centered Perspective Of History

1st Edition 1989
2nd Revised updated version © January 1994
    ©Tsehloane Keto/Research Associates School Times Publications

ISBN - 09483 901 31

Library Of Congress Catalogue Card Number 93-86120

All Rights Reserved.
©1994 Research Associates School Times Publications/Karnak House
Published in USA and Britain
by Research Associates School Times Publications and Karnak House
300 Westbourne Park Road
London W11 1EH
and 751 East 75th Street Chicago IL 60619

Distributed in the USA and Canada by
Frontline Distribution International, Inc.
751 East 75th Street
Chicago, IL 60619
(312) 651-9888
Fax (312) 651-9850

Second Revised Edition
©
Copyright 1993
C. Tsehloane Keto

All Rights Reserved

DEDICATED

TO

THE GENERATION OF

ADIKA, ANWAR, BRIAN, DIKENGKENG, FRED, FRED III, HARVEY JR., HOLO, JEREL, KEDIBONE, LEBOHANG, LEFA, LEFANYANA, LENTSWE, LERATO, MAKGODU, MATSEHLAWNE, MODIBEDI, POELANO, RHONDA, SELLO, SHEELITA, STEPHANIE, THABO, THAPELO, TIA, TLOLISO.

Table of Contents

Acknowledgements 6

1. Introduction 12

Part I. The Africa Centered Perspective: A Description 29

2. Centers, Geography and Language 32

3. Social Sciences and History 42

4. Hegemonic Europe Centered Perspective 50

5. Non-Hegemonic Europe Centered Perspective 56

6. The Africa Centered Perspective and Gender 65

Part II. Applying The Africa Centered Perspective 73
A. Concept Building 73

7. The Concept of the Third World 75

8. Marxist Theory and an Africa Centered Perspective 80

9. African American History 90

10. South African History 107

11. Conclusion 118

NOTES 129

GLOSSARY 146

SELECT BIBLIOGRAPHY 153

LIST OF MAPS

Global Polycentered Perspective 27

Europe Centered Historical Movement 64

Africa Centered Historical Movement 72

Creation of the Global Pluriverse 117

Acknowledgements

This publication has benefitted from the criticism of the faculty of the Department of African American Studies at Temple University. Dr. Molefi Kete Asante and Dr. Abu Abarry made valuable comments that I have incorporated in the text. Graduate and undergraduate students who used the book in their classes over the last two years have made useful recommendations that have improved the lucidity of the abstract discussion in part one. Some colleagues and students challenged the existence of a nonhegemonic Europe centered outlook in the contemporary human sciences. Although I appreciate the historical basis for this concern, I believe that there has always been the <u>theoretical possibility</u> of such a viewpoint. The historical record bears this out. Even in the heyday of hegemonic Eurocentricism and European imperialism, there were European intellectuals who advocated viewpoints critical of hegemonic tendencies within the Eurocentric framework. These nonhegemonists may not have represented the dominant "intellectual trend" of the time in the beginning, but, over time, this perspective within Eurocentric scholarship has enlarged its voice and as a result has left open the theoretical possibility of a common ground with a nonhegemonic Africa centered perspective. In this publication, I have purposely combined quotations from Africa centered works with citations from Europe centered works in order to demonstrate in practice the existence of an "antihegemonic" common ground.

There are many people inside and outside Africa who deserve credit for enhancing the ideas I have expressed throughout this publication. The Africa centered paradigm and the perspective that derives from it is the result of a mixture of study, reflection, social influences and personal experiences. The ideas that I have articulated in this publication most certainly did not emerge full blown in my head all by themselves. I have shared in the thinking of countless minds on three continents. A wide and diverse circle of people who were my teachers, my university instructors, my mentors, my friends, my associates, my acquaintances, my colleagues and members of my family in the African sense contributed to my ideas and my thinking. I would especially like to give credit to all the students I taught in Lesotho, Zambia and the United States. Although I cannot list all of their names, I do wish to thank them for their collective contribution to the ideas in this publication. I say to them "Le ka moso baheso" and "Asante sana."

I acknowledge with deep gratitude my indebtedness to the ideas of my parents Lentsoe Victor Tsehloane and Naniwe Catherine [Mazibu] Tsehloane, my aunt Lerato Emily [Tsehloane] Baholo and her husband Ebenezer Baholo, my grandfather Samson Letlea Tsehloane and my grandmother Makgodu Josephine [Moshoeshoe] Tsehloane and my brother Nicholas Tsehloane. Since they are joined with the immortal part of our family, this publication represents part of their precious legacy to future generations. I am because they were.

I also recognize the inspiration, assistance and encouragement of my sister Lerato Constance Tsehloane, my cousin Cuthbert Mazibu, my friends Wesley Mbulelo Nakin, Graham Motsilili, Rampa Moshoeshoe, Amanda Moshoeshoe, Lefu-lesele Ralake and my special friend Moeketsi, all South Africans. I thank them for being there for me at critical times in my life even when we were separated by great distances of space and decades of time.

The collective support of all the people who played a part in my development as a person driven by a positive force has nurtured me into the person that I am. Through their practical examples I have come to develop a value and a pride in myself that does not require to be sustained by disrespect for the pride and value of others nor to belittle those who were different from me. Their words and actions confirmed for me a deep commitment to the simple proposition that my personal dignity is like a ship that is only able to stay afloat on a sea of respect for the dignity of others. I have also appreciated an expanded consciousness that came from a perspective that acknowledged the contribution of "diverse others" in the definition and realization of self.

As I read daily about intractable "people to people" problems in Africa, Europe, Asia and America, I become convinced more than ever that the worst error of principle we make towards other people is when we condemn and "punish people for being the children of their parents." The principle of interpersonal and intrapersonal harmony rests on the basic notion of respect for the `personhood' of others; a tenet that is central to the ethics of "Botho or Ubuntu" which bears a striking resemblance to the principle of righteousness called "Maat" found in ancient Kemet. This notion of Botho/Ubuntu is understood by many in the African world. I hold firmly to this ethical framework which is based on those aspects of the African worldview that celebrates diversity without imposing hierarchy.

For this revised edition I thank Nadia Kravchenko

of the College of Arts and Sciences at Temple University who performed her wonderful magic to produce the finished quality copy for publication.

My twin sons Lefa and Lefanyana, contributed with their patience in this endeavor of endless revisions. The family that adopted me in the period of my personal crisis made up of Isoke and her sons, Anwar and Adika, had it worse because they had to put up with my absent-mindedness like the time I started pulling off a parking space with Michael's foot still on the pavement outside the car! I thank them for suffering with me through those hazards of excessive contemplation!

All errors and imperfections that remain in this publication remain my sole responsibility.

C. Tsehloane Keto
Gloucester Township,
New Jersey
August 1993

1. Introduction

The Africa centered perspective of history is closely associated with what we can call an Afrocentric paradigm. A paradigm is a model or a pattern based on certain common assumptions. The Afrocentric paradigm in turn rests on a basic principle of common sense. That basic principle holds that there is profound intellectual merit in treating the continent of Africa as a geo-cultural starting point, a 'center' so to speak, that serves as an axiological reference point for the purpose of gathering, ordering and interpreting information about African people at home on the continent and throughout those parts of the world where African people have formed culturally significant communities. African people become subjects and makers of their own history when we employ the Afrocentric paradigm as our primary foundation for creating theoretical tools of analysis. Africans are not and cannot be peripheral dwellers in somebody else's unfolding historical panorama. Perspective implies a viewpoint and every intellectual gatherer occupies an identifiable center or location which provides an operational perspective that, when honestly pursued, affects the focus of gathered social data in all the human sciences. Scholars who are intellectual gatherers cannot study the actions of people on this planet without reference to a location or "a center" that is either overt or covert. The human sciences depend on perspective and honest scholarship demands that the perspective be made explicit and publicly acknowledged. Those who deny or conceal their perspective and their center are either seriously uninformed or in pursuit of intellectual hegemony for the center and perspective they espouse.

The African continent has a unique place in early human history which requires that I define the limit I will place on the operational meaning of the term "African" as I employ it in the narrative that follows. Fossil, biological and linguistic research has indicated that humanity, with its diverse languages and cultures originated on the African continent. If we accept a monogenetic origin for humanity, then all people of the world are of "African origin." In one sense then, all the world's people can lay claim to being of "African descent." The consequences of this realization are profound. One cannot be Africa centered and "racist" or "purist" at the same time. Think of a tree with roots, stem and branches. A branch can dream of purity from other branches. This would be an illusion of course since they are all connected to the stem and ultimately the roots. The stem and roots cannot entertain such an illusion first because the roots join the stem which in turn feeds the branches. Sections of humanity can entertain "illusions" of purity but Africans cannot since they are connected to an earlier unity of humanity. The differences that are biological become significant in terms of "post-African" cultural formations for peoples outside Africa. The unity and diversity of the world's people is dialectical. Cultures formed within the stream of time are in themselves socially significant.

In this publication I will use the term "African" in a historically specific and culturally restricted sense. I have recognized human groupings according to continents: I refer to Europeans, Asians and First Americans. I will therefore call African, those branches of the human family which remained on the ancestral continent after other branches who were to become the progenitors of the other biological, cultural and linguistic branches of the human family had left the "home" continent 200,000 years or so ago. If this demarcation appears vague in biological terms, it also betrays my preference for a cultural basis for human classification. People may differ biologically but it is culture that designates those differences that become socially relevant in history. Linda James Meyer has outlined elements of an African worldview. This worldview, she argues, is holistic and humanistic. These two elements alone place the Africa centered perspective in a non-racist mode.

For those Africans who remained and continued to built up their social heritage into cultures centered on the historical experience of the "home continent," the Africa centered perspective makes it easier to explain and to understand by way of "culture" those social patterns that have marked African choices in the area of coexistence with the environment, the institutional patterns that have characterized the actions of African people in people-to-people relations and those intellectual choices and styles that Africans have used to construct knowledge systems that have borne the signature of African thoughts and African motifs in the past and in the present.

As a theoretical position that emerges from the Afrocentric paradigm, a reflection of an active agent for praxical change within a re-emerging school of knowledge formation in the twentieth century and a tool for analytical investigation in the human sciences, the Africa centered perspective encourages human "science" practitioners who analyze the social phenomena that exist within, and the social phenomena that impinge upon, the world where African people live, to critique the way they approach their study of historical Africans in two distinct ways.

First, researchers have to clarify, at the level at which they form theory, how they view knowledge and its validity, and how they explain the relationship between the knowing subject--the person who knows--and the information that is known. This is the level of the epistemological perspective that is critical. The Cartesian dichotomy makes it impossible to bridge the gap between the knower and the known. The Asantian position denies the existence of the dichotomy in the Afrocentric paradigm and concludes that knowing itself is always a subject created exercise.

The human scientists also have to indicate, as a matter of practical concern, whether their epistemology proceeds as a logical discourse, that is, one that emphasizes either the unilinear sequential relations of propositions and statements to one another or adheres to curvilinear polyconnected statements. The latter position could also pursue a hermeneutic discourse, that is, one that unfolds vistas of new information through paradigm shifts since new paradigms unlock previously unopened doors to new knowledge and insight. The researchers may also choose to employ, interactively, multiple forms of discourse. Once readers can 'place a fix' on the center and type of discourse that scholars use, it is easier for them to anticipate where the authors of scholarly discourse are leading them.

On a second and less abstract level, investigators should openly specify, when they begin to apply methods derived from chosen methodologies and theories onto concrete situations, the geographical and cultural location that they adopt as the "primordial cultural core." Often this "hidden center," so to speak, represents the underlying premise from which researchers draw values and priorities with which they fashion the concepts that will be used to observe, judge and interpret world events as well as derivative human developments that cluster around those events. In other words human scientists are encouraged to openly specify the particular regional "center" on the globe which provides the fulcrum on which they anchor historical and therefore human meaning and interpretation. We need to know the center to understand how concepts about people and past events are created, expanded and sustained. This enables us to distinguish "totalizing" concepts that are hegemonic from concepts that are frankly identified as sectional and therefore nonhegemonic. A good example of a nonhegemonic perspective is found in the principles associated with what Western philosophers call cultural relativism.[1]

An Africa centered perspective further helps us to obtain intellectual clarity and honesty about the processes described in the preceding paragraphs, by accomplishing two things.

First, it begins with Africa as the historical core from which to build the narrative and the analysis of the experiences of people in Africa and peoples of African descent throughout the world, the significant regional cultural groupings that have emerged as well as the related but diversifying cultural cores that have appeared in history. These new derivative centers or fragments from original African cultures are continually being formed in history. These become vital "centers" of local focus and crosscultural rejuvenation such as those we find in the United States, Jamaica, Brazil and Trinidad. These derivative "centers" or cultural fragments are legitimate in their own right for the construction of new knowledge as long as investigating scholars remember that the new centers with all their uniqueness, ultimately relate their core features back to a historical center on the mother continent of Africa.

Second and equally significant, the Africa centered perspective seeks to bring to the interpretation and understanding of global events those "humanistic" values about being a person whose historical origins are traceable, in part or in whole, to African roots. A West African saying describes the value of connectedness to a "time-space center" in these sobering expressions:

> If you do not know where you are
> or where you have been,
> you cannot know where you are going -
> and, if you do not know where you
> are going,
> any road will take you there.

Marcus Garvey was to indicate that a people without knowledge of its history was like a tree without roots which could be swayed in any direction by the prevailing winds of the time.

CATEGORIZING KNOWLEDGE:

The categories of knowledge about people that emerged in the "Western construction" of university systems have diversified into what we call the "social sciences" on one hand, as well as the value centered "humanities" on the other. Both categories are closely and symbiotically related to the study of the past. In many respects, the social sciences and the humanities as human sciences are specialized forms of history. In order to do so we have to define history as a special manifestation of "public memory." In the context of history as public memory, literature, drama, theater and poetry are creative forms of that "public memory" that effectively store emotion and feeling. Despite this power of "creativity" and "re-creation," these fields of learning still retain their character as repositories of public memory. They can be profitably consulted by later generations to recall the past in a way that is different from that of the narrative form found in many historical accounts.

As we currently conceptualize them, the humanities as a subject area of study embrace values and celebrate the vital role of centered values in people's lives. Humanities as a result stay true to the centers from which they originated. African literature, African American poetry, English literature, French poetry, Chinese poetry and Italian literature are unambiguous fields tied to the creative energies of particular peoples at specific points in history. Major problems arise when canons of literary criticism are constructed from one center and used clumsily to judge literature from different centers. "Center" hegemony in such a case replaces honest scholarship and imposes a form of "discipline" control.

In the last one hundred years, some practitioners of the increasingly overlapping "social sciences" have toyed, unsuccessfully in my estimation, with the theoretical pretension of transcending values and uncovering hidden "universal laws" of social change. These scholars were too impatient, and too arrogant, to wait, analyze and explain change from different parts of the world after it comes. They have been unsuccessful because they have singularly failed to predict the most awesome radical developments of the twentieth century before they occurred in Eastern Europe, Asia or Africa.

When we claim that history encompasses the social sciences and the humanities, we have to justify the primacy of history. Our experience indicates that analysis and creative production always occur in the context of a place [space] and a time. Therefore creative production is in the sphere of history the moment it is 'completed'. Drama, poetry and dance have the singular power of creative re-enactment again and again. In the end however they end up in the sphere of the past which is the domain of historical studies.

History, at best, separates the "first fundamental reality" of a people's existence, namely, the past, from the second fundamental reality of existence, namely, the present. The third element which completes the time triangle is the future. The future is a special case because it exists only in the vision that people have about it and in the plans they make for it. Yet those plans are made and actualized in the context of the present.

A poetic rendition of this triangular relationship of the past, the present and the future is superbly conveyed in the phrase:

'the present is a room furnished by the past
and lit by the future.'

People always act in the present which then becomes the past from which they can learn. They are always motivated by objectives and goals that lie in the future. The relationship of these three points of the time triangle are critical to the successful creation and sustenance of a meaningful historical consciousness.

History as a conceptualized field of the study of the past, is different from "total history." History in the restrictive sense of a "reconstructed past" automatically implies that it is a selective and interpreted history which is the handiwork of scholars, dead and alive. Only "total history" encompasses "the sum total of what happened in the past--what was done by billions of people over millions of years in trillions of occurrences".[2]

Historians do not even attempt to write about "total history" except indirectly through attempts to create a metatheory that will explain the "structure" of history. Instead, scholars creatively reconstruct the history of the relatively remote past using distinctive methodologies of research, theories of interpretation, and styles of presentation which all revolve around written and unwritten sets of reclaimable records. Scholars engaged in this process make countless choices about what is significant and what is trivial; and through theories of interpretation, determine how the selected sets of information relate to one another. This necessary selection process has in the past frequently led to an implicit, creeping [and sometimes unconscious] use of ethnocentric values and gender bias as if they were universally determined. In the specific case of the study of African peoples in different parts of the world, in the last five hundred years, that bias has usually reflected the result of employing frameworks of analysis based on a hegemonic Europe centered perspective.

There is a proper place for Europe-centered, Asia centered, and America centered analyses of Africa and

Africans in the historical perspectives of world literature in order to counteract any overly parochialized view of Africa and Africans that might emerge in Africa centered analyses, but that in turn should call for a reciprocal need for an Africa centered, Asia centered and America centered historical analyses of Europe and Europeans to prevent similarly parochialized views of Europe and Europeans that might emerge from a Europe centered analysis. The same would apply to Asia centered and America centered analyses regard Asians and Americans. Otherwise we will still be dealing with an unequal terrain of intellectual exchange favoring Europe centered knowledge. We will be engaging in knowledge formation that is less than "center diverse" in its perspective in the process of creating "global consciousness of history."

However, a more critical contribution to this "global consciousness" about history in the context of Africa can be made by developing more historical literature in the 1990s and beyond, that reflects a diverse, insightful and informative Africa centered historical perspective of Africa, Africans and the descendants of Africans just as there exists at present an impressive array of literature that reflects an informative and insightful Europe centered historical perspective of

Europe, Europeans and descendants of Europeans. Currently, the very intellectual framework of African and African American historiography leans too heavily on conceptual products of a Europe centered perspective. The time, has come to recreate a broader framework and to redress the balance in global scholarship by writing more books and articles based on an Africa centered perspective of history. The Africa centered framework can also act as a primary filter in the study of Africa, Africans and peoples of African descent.[3]

The Africa Centered Perspective and Afrocentricity:

Afrocentricity represents a philosophical position that originates from an Africa centered point of reference. Asante describes it as "the most complete philosophical totalization of the African being-at-the-center of her or his existence." In another context Asante also designated Afrocentricity as a facet of "centrism" and defined it as

> groundedness which allows the student of
> human culture investigating Africa phenomena
> to view the world from the standpoint
> of the African.[4]

The Africa centered perspective that we explore here is confined to the study of the past and contends that information about the past makes better sense when we understand the framework around which it is wrapped. The information may come encased in a Eurocentric, Asiacentric, Americacentric or Afrocentric framework. The Africa centered perspective of history will portray the insights that can be achieved by employing an Afrocentric paradigm.

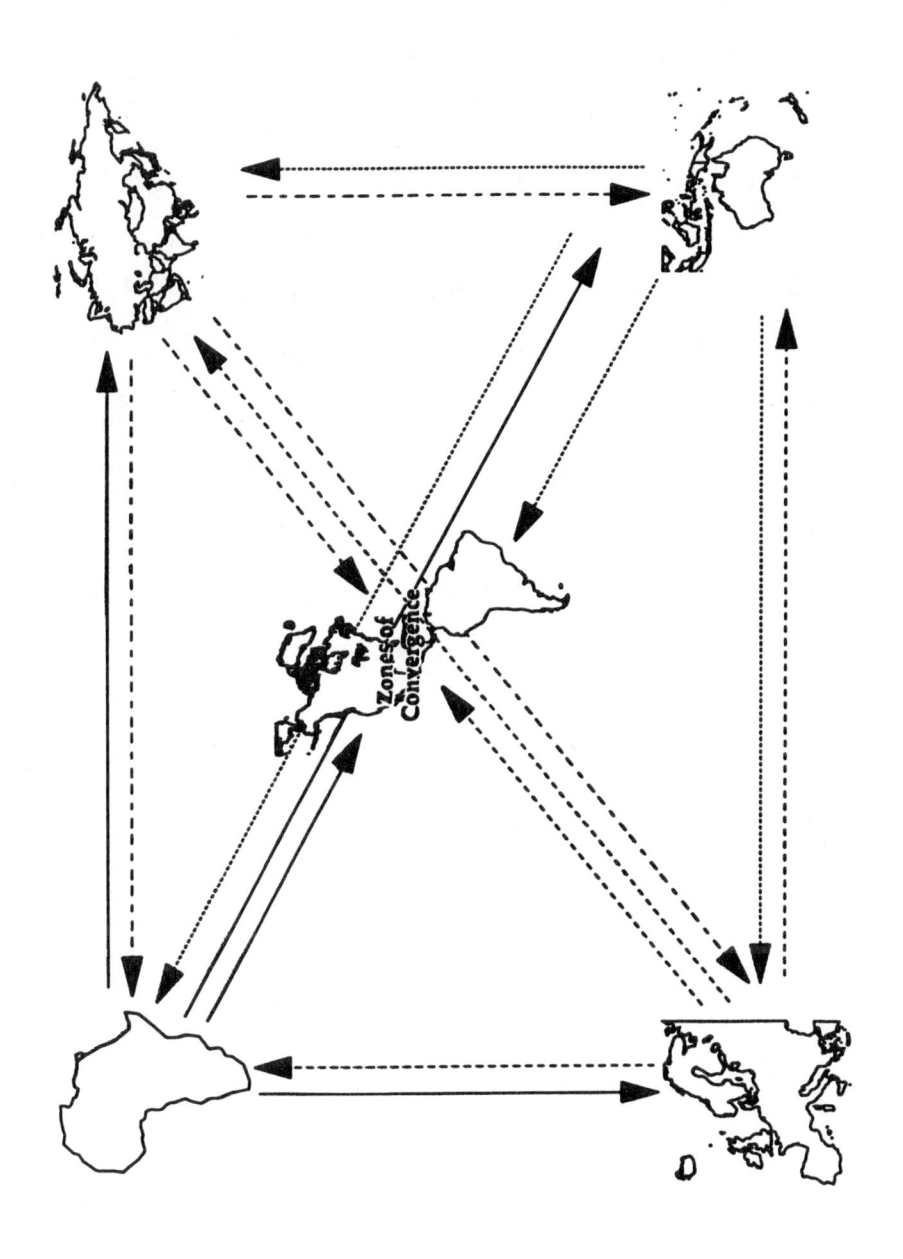

Global Polycentered Perspective

Part I. The Africa Centered Perspective: A Description

In the pages that follow, I will portray the Africa centered perspective of history in phases. Each phase will set the foundation for understanding the phases that follow.

A. In the first phase, I will consider the importance of centers and show how

[1] certain concepts in Geography and

[2] the use of European languages constantly strengthen a Europe centered perspective and what can be done to correct this center imbalance for a multicutural world.

B. In the second phase, I will briefly review the relations between the "human sciences" and history in the context of continent centered frameworks. Then I will explain the meaning I prefer for the translation of the term `science' in the human sciences.

C. In the third phase, I will describe the difference between a hegemonic Europe centered perspective that originates from the days of European imperialism and contrast it with the intellectually healthier nonhegemonic Europe centered perspective.

D. In the fourth and final phase, I will outline what I

consider to be the critical elements of an Africa centered perspective of history and how it should interface with both class and gender issues.

Be warned that some of the discussion may appear to be a little abstract in the beginning. The reader should bear with me as we go through this discussion. I need to construct a solid theoretical foundation in order to explain an Africa centered perspective and the Afrocentric paradigm adequately. The discussion in the second part of this publication regarding African American and African history is without value and has no leg to stand on without the theoretical base of the first part of the publication. As you read the historical examples in the second part, the need for abstract discussion in the first part will become obvious.

2. Centers, Geography and Language

The implicit and explicit conceptual consequence of the "geographical framework" for the Africa centered perspective is the easiest part of the theoretical paradigm to demonstrate. What I will discuss may appear elementary to those scholars who already operate on advanced levels of awareness in the "centrist theory" of human knowledge, but it provides a necessary foundation of concrete examples to subsequent abstract discussion for those who are beginning the climb to understand "centered knowledge." As many scholars of Afrocentric theory such as Molefi Kete Asante, Wade Nobles, Na'im Akbar, Maulana Karenga, Jacob Carruthers, Ngugi Wa Thiongo and Dona Marimba Richards have attested in their published writings and speeches, the world as it is currently conceptualized in many learning institutions around the world is generally cast in a Europe centered perspective that is grounded on a Eurocentric paradigm. In Europe and in areas of the world colonized only by peoples of European descent, this perspective makes a great deal of sense and is therefore not a major obstacle in knowledge creation, knowledge acquisition and knowledge transmission.[5]

However we should also add a cautionary note. In regions of the planet where people from different parts of the world have came together, areas which I regard as "zones of human confluence," the Europe centered perspective, by itself creates confusion and distortion because it employs a "hegemonic" Eurocentric framework which is socially and culturally inadequate in a polycentric milieu. At the very least, a framework of analysis in such areas should also incorporate other perspectives to provide a truly "plural perspective" of human developments in those regions.

The intellectual dominance of a Europe centered perspective of knowledge around the world reflects the attendant effects, on the growth of global knowledge, of the expansion of a European political economy and its military power into other parts of the world and the consequent establishment of European centered intellectual hegemony on most, but not all, learning centers of the world since 1500. This state of affairs is neither new in world history nor unexpected. Those who become politically or economically "dominant," control resources and exercise power, consciously or unconsciously, tend to encourage everyone else to view the state of affairs, even within the same community, through a perspective that is in harmony with their interests, supportive of the status quo and conducive to their retention of social advantage.

In two areas of geography it is easy to document the Europe centered nature of concepts that masquerade as "universal concepts" in that field. Lines of longitude used to map out international time, are most convenient for Western Europe. The phrase "Greenwich Meantime" and the numbering of lines of longitude with a zero in Western Europe are two minor indicators of this centeredness. Lines of longitude vividly demonstrate the dominance of Western Europe in the construction of global time zones. It should not be surprising to discover that the most inconvenient consequences of this international time zone arrangement are to be found in the Pacific, the most distant place from Western Europe "longitudinally speaking."

The second series of clues is found in the names given to the various "regions" of the world. The "Middle East," and the "Far East" in Asia are designations that derive their reference point from their location and distance from the European continent. The "Middle East" in an Asia centered perspective should be called "South West Asia." Similarly, in the United States, the "Midwest" and the "Far

West" reflect the patterns of human settlement by America's immigrants of Anglo-European descent who came to dominate the continent after the Mexican war of 1846-1848. In South Africa, Ciskei, Transkei and Transvaal reproduce the patterns of European movements and migrations. The names of towns, regions, mountains and rivers echo the European center of the naming process: New England, New London, East London, Berlin, Paris, New Orleans, New Jersey and New York. The result of accident and history creates a conceptualization of geography that is later justified because it has become conventional and/or international. This conceptualization often peripheralizes the indigenous inhabitants by using terms such as the "Wilderness" to describe parts of a continent that have not been settled by Europeans.

The still favorite term Non-Western to refer to the majority of the world's people is another indicator. It replaces the old terms of Non-European and Non-White which reinforced the definition of the majority as a negative of a white minority. This is hegemonic Europe centered concept formation at its worst.

Another interesting display of the dominance of a Europe centered perspective is to be found in the continued preference of Mercator projection maps [1569] which distort the relative size of the land masses of the world in favor of the northern tier in which Europe is located despite the presence of the Peters projection since 1980 which shows the true relative size of the land masses of the world and makes the size of the southern tier conceptually visible.

English, the international language of science in the contemporary world, being a western European language, automatically carries within its internal construction, the Europe centered bias. This admission is not in itself an insurmountable part of the problem because language is malleable and can be modified to reflect the experience of those who use it as the case of Ebonics or "Black English" within American English and the use of English by African writers like Chinu Achebe and Wole Soyinka demonstrate. The major part of the problem in language use, for history and the human sciences, arises when people who use the language claim universal validity and application for the parochial aspects of its connotations, thereby falsely depicting as universal that which is legitimately parochial or regional.[6]

Language is such an important part of communicating about Africa, Africans and the descendants of Africans in the

Americas, Europe and Asia that when we employ the criterion of European language use as an organizing principle of understanding African reality we distort the African reality. We should always clarify the implications of what we are doing with such a venture. We can arrange the study of Africa, the Caribbean or the Americas as Anglophone, Francophone, Lusophone or Hispanic areas. But when we do this we consciously select a Europe centered perspective of the people we are studying. There is indeed a great wealth of Anglophone African literature, Francophone African literature and Lusophone African literature. These literatures can be studied as part of English literature, French literature or Portuguese literature--thereby adopting a Europe centered perspective. The common, decisive and unifying thread in this instance is the European language used to express African thoughts. However when we study, integrate and analyze this same literature with literature in Arabic, Yoruba, Akan, Wolof, Kiswahili, Amharic, ChiBemba, Hausa, Zezuru, IsiZulu and SeSotho, we are closer to employing a truly Africa centered perspective of the literature because what binds the literatures together is the African's experience and not simply the medium of expressing that experience. This is part of cultural identity confusion.

The Europe centered basis of self-identity adopted by Africans certainly shocked African American scholars. W.E.B. Du Bois and Rayford W. Logan were pleasantly surprised when the "French" deputy from Senegal, Blaisé Diagne, informed Africans and African Americans gathered in Paris for the Second Pan African Conference in 1921 that he was "French first, and a Negro African second." That continuing ambiguity about the double consciousness of Francophone Africans who straddle the Europe centered and Africa centered perspectives explains the intellectual chasm that existed between two outstanding Senegalese intellectuals, the Africa centered historian Cheikh Anta Diop and the sometimes Europe centered and sometimes Africa centered poet and past president Leopold Senghor. Another attempt to reconcile this ambiguity of a Europe centered "cosmopolitan" consciousness and an Africa centered consciousness by the Negritude school was sometimes done by surrendering `reason' to Europe in order to preserve `feeling' for Africa.

W.E.B. Du Bois was more honest in 1903 and confronted the "center" issue when he wrote of the "double consciousness" among African Americans. He described this consciousness as the "second sight in this American

World--a world which yields [the African American] . . . no true self-consciousness, but only lets . . . [the African American] see himself [/herself] through the revelation of the other world."

Du Bois then proceeded to explain the dilemma of the African American intellectual in these memorable words:

> It is a peculiar sensation, this double consciousness, this sense of always looking at one's self through the eyes of others . . . One ever feels . . . [this] two-ness- . . . two souls, two thoughts, two unreconciled strivings; two warring ideals in one dark body, whose dogged strength alone keeps it from being torn asunder.
> The history of the ... [African American] is the history of this strife-this longing to ... merge [this] ... double self into a better and truer self. In this merging he[/she] wishes neither of the older selves to be lost . . . He[/She] simply wishes to make it possible for a . . . [person] to be both . . . [African] and . . . American

without . . . having the door opportunity closed . . . in his[/her] face. 7

This attempt to reconcile the "two centers" of knowledge about themselves can be noted in the writings of many African Americans such as David Walker, Maria Stewart, Frederick Douglass, Martin Delany, Henry Mcneil Turner, Langston Hughes, Marcus Garvey, Malcolm X and Zora Neale Hurston. Centers provide the basis on which frameworks are created. In turn the frameworks generate the concepts that order the understanding of social reality. Those who know more than one center understand the conflict of the frameworks and are sensitive to the diversity of humanity. Those who are unaware of the multiplicity of centers or choose to ignore other centers, often believe that their center is the only center that makes sense in world history. That cultural arrogance often leads to human tragedy of major proportions.

This signal issue of "centers" has been addressed in a slightly different form by Samuel P. Huntington in his article on "The Clash of Civilizations?" Huntington argues that the next major foci of conflict will be in the clash of civilizations which he defines in terms of religious and ethnic groups. "A civilization," he contends, "is . . . the highest cultural grouping of people and the broadest level of cultural identity people have short of that which distinguishes humans from other species." This way of viewing the world establishes two zones in Europe and three in Asia. He downplays African although he acknowledges a possible African civilization as one of eight civilizations. His article is important because he places "culture" at the center of future world conflict. But the premises are hegemonic as conflict arises out of the need of one civilization to dominate other civilizations.[8]

3. Social Sciences and History

The meaning of the term social science as it is used in the late twentieth century has undergone subtle changes. This change of meaning has fueled misleading implications. Some social theorists who have used it have pushed its definition closer to the narrower connotations of the way it is used as it applies to the natural sciences. It is equally ironic that the "authorities" who are frequently quoted from the nineteenth century to bolster the claims of social science often attached a broader meaning to the word "science" than its Twentieth Century users. Then, the meaning of science was nearer to the meaning embodied in the translation of its latin origin "Sciens" [infinitive-"scire"] which means "knowledge." A "scientist" was a "scholar," one who pursued knowledge systematically rather than people with white coats working in laboratories or around computers, telescopes, nuclear reactors and frogs. "Scientific" once meant "systematic," "thorough" and "well thought out" before it became an instrument in the hands of `positivists' and `materialists' for uncovering the hidden "universal laws" of history, social change and human development to be used for social engineering purposes.

The underlying problem with this "natural science" model of science is that the social sciences and history as a package of "human sciences" are fundamentally different from the natural sciences. John Lukacs provides an excellent explanation for this signal difference. The reason for this difference, he argues, is

> because the knowledge that people have of other people is less accurate and different from the knowledge that people have of animals, vegetables [and] minerals. ·

The way we acquire and organize the knowledge we have about other people and the way we acquire and organize the knowledge we have about animals, plants and inanimate objects is fundamentally dissimilar because a different kind of experimentation is possible in the case of things which is not available in the case of people.

In regard to the social sciences we should also note that, in contradistinction to history, they reclaim their information from records about people that are fairly recent. Since they operate with an abbreviated temporal dimension, they represent a form of history which has to rely heavily on sophisticated theory and methodology in order to compensate for the absence of "time depth" in the social data that is available. With a narrow time frame at their disposal, social sciences have been accused at times of substituting emphasis on the quantity of data available rather than the quality of the data needed. In other cases, the social sciences do rely on the findings of historians to reach definitive conclusions about how people behave over long periods of time and to provide confirmation of societal patterns based on long term observations. Some social scientists of the twentieth century have, however, gone one step further and attempted to build sophisticated theories of explanation that can predict people's behavior. This way of thinking is represented by concepts such as "social engineering."

Some social scientists often claim, and with

some justification, that history is no more than "a retrospective social science." The close relationship of history to the social sciences and the increasing overlap in scope among the social science "disciplines" suggests

[1] that the social sciences and history are two sides of the knowledge "reconstruction" coin and

[2] that a radical overhaul of how social science "disciplines" are conceptualized even in the "Western tradition" is now overdue after a century of growth and proliferation.[10]

Given the close relationship between history and the social sciences, an Africa centered perspective of history helps to break new ground in the human sciences by providing an important alternative historical framework in the necessary process of refocusing, formulating and fine tuning knowledge about Africans in the social sciences. This alternative framework suggests novel ways to re-organize the conceptual baskets that house our knowledge about people. The Africa centered perspective is in turn continuously affected by theoretical and applications developments in the Afrocentric, Eurocentric, Asiacentric and

Americacentric social sciences theories that are a precursor to "multicentered" human sciences.

Finally, in arguing the case for an Africa centered perspective of history we also undertake the task of liberating the unwitting intellectual prisoners who worship "blind universal history" as it applies to Africa and Africans. We save them from self-deception by gently reminding them that what they worship as universal history ". . . is, . . ., as much a product of the mind of the historian who wrote it as it is the product of the actions of the people who actually lived it." In other words, we warn everyone that none of us can avoid the implicit influence of the historians' "perspective" derived from some specific center in the history we read. Most of those who claim to speak for "universal" history actually embrace historical knowledge cast in a hegemonic Eurocentric framework. When I insist on this unveiling of a Eurocentric framework, I do not deny the validity of history in its properly restricted context with involved "center" bias made explicit. I seek to demystify history's unqualified significance for the human "science" practitioners of the Twenty First

Century.[11]

The same John Lukacs we referred to earlier develops a critique of history that directly makes a strong case for creating the intellectual space in academia for an Africa centered perspective when he describes the elements that have created the crisis in history and the social sciences in America. Lukacs argues that the very nature of human knowledge is circumscribed by the "limitations that give it special validity and meaning." "These limitations have now been recognized--and experimentally proven," he maintains,"--in [quantum] physics, in the study of matter itself; [although] it will be a long time [he argues] before the meaning of this is accepted, even by physicists." Only after that he writes, "will a new and unitary conception of man's relationship to the universe crystallize, superseding the Cartesian division of object and subject and the increasingly corroded ideal of `objectivity'."

Lukacs then concludes that in the study of history and human societies "description must have priority over definition, narrative over abstraction, words over numbers" because the method, purpose and practicality of our knowledge of things depend[s] on <u>accuracy</u>" while the "... purpose of our knowledge of other human beings is <u>understanding</u>, the kind... which... is both more or less than certainty."[12]

The fallacy of so-called "objectivity" in history is dismissed in a summary manner by Maulana Karenga's definition and description of history as people centered. For Karenga:

> History is the struggle and record of humans in the process of humanizing the world, i.e., shaping it in their own image and interests. To shape the world in a human image is to give it a human form and character and to shape it in human interests... [is] to make it serve humans rather than threaten, deform and destroy them.

"African or Black history then," argues Karenga, "is the struggle and record of Africans in the process of Africanizing the world, i.e., shaping it in their own image and interests."[13]

I agree substantially with Lukacs' critique and Karenga's centered definition. I find an important element missing in Lukacs' discussion, namely, the historical dimension. That dimension would demonstrate that the origins of the current conceptual crisis and confusion are to be found partially in the uncritical assumptions of an hegemonic Europe centered perspective which made the human experiences of the rest of the world invisible in history. It is this experience that Karenga reintroduces.

The hegemonic and totalizing effect of a Eurocentric historical perspective was demonstrated by Hegel when he proclaimed the "end of history" in the nineteenth century. Ironically, an Asian American repeated the same theme in equally totalizing and hegemonic Eurocentric terms when he regarded the end of the Communism versus Capitalism conflict or Cold War as the "end of history" rather than the end of Eurocentric ideological war.

4. Hegemonic Europe Centered Perspective

This hegemonic Eurocentric perspective was the most prevalent type of Europe centered perspective in the last 100 years. This perspective, reflecting European imperialism, indiscriminately imposed the parochial aspects of the European experience on the rest of the world and tied it to a belief in "white supremacy." The perspective made implicit claims of universality for what were only legitimate Europe centered values. No indepth comparative studies were undertaken in other parts of the world to verify whether the European experience lived up to its claims of universality. The term "comparative studies" was used loosely by practitioners of this perspective to judge the rest of the world using preferences that were based on a totalizing Europe centered framework. That however was only one part of the problematic. This Eurocentric framework was also subsumed under implicit rather than explicit terms. The terminology employed emphasized phrases and words such as `international,' `global' and `cosmopolitan' to represent transnational

European trends and developments as if they were universal. Scholars from cultures outside the European experience sometimes internalized this Eurocentric perspective in studying their own cultures.

The distribution of the world's population according to 1990 population estimates demonstrates just how distortive the conclusions drawn from the assumptions of a hegemonic Europe centered perspective can be in a global context. Let us look at these figures:

WORLD POPULATION FIGURES

CONTINENT	%	POPULATION IN MILLIONS
ASIA	61.6	2,877
AFRICA	12.5	583
EUROPE	10.6	493
NORTH AND MIDDLE AMERICA	8.3	386
CARIBBEAN AND SOUTH AMERICA	6.7	311
AUSTRALIA AND NEW ZEALAND	.4	18
* TOTALS	100.1	4668[14]

According to any interpretation of these figures,

the peoples of Asia constitute two thirds of humanity and may have constituted the majority of the world's people for the last four centuries. Even if we include peoples of European descent in the other land areas to the figures for Europe the effect is still the same. Figures on Africa can also be augmented by numbers from the African diaspora in Asia and the Americas to a total that is close to a billion people. These figures question the representative nature of the European experience alone even when that experience later percolates to other parts of the globe. The figures provide prima facie evidence that on the whole, peoples of continents outside of the Asian side of the Asia-European land mass, make up varying sizes of the world's numerical <u>minorities</u> no matter how one slices the world's population pie. So the European experience cannot be representative on the basis of numbers or culture.

However, we can legitimately argue that different

regions of the world have become centers that have evolved distinctively diverse cultures. These regions as centers are entitled to develop paradigms of knowledge that reflect the perspectives of the region's qualitatively significant human cultures, histories and experiences. Recognition of these multiple experiences and the perspectives that grow out of them provide an opportunity to test the applicability of theories that attempt to explain the varied dimensions of the human experience. Through true comparative analysis, studies would separate those observations and findings that are 'universal' in the sense that they apply to and explain all comparable social situations from those that are particular and unique to one "center." Such a drawn out process would lay a legitimate groundwork for "pluriversal" or "multicentered" social science theories for the Twenty First Century which would have drawn their conclusions by extrapolating from global rather than regional trends.

This diverse 'social data base' would provide the most plausible case for 'pluriversal social sciences' if such intellectual enterprises are at all possible. The trouble in the last hundred years was that studies about the rest of the world were overly influenced and often distorted by theories and conclusions drawn from studies based on a "minority" of the world's families, a "minority" of the world's women, a "minority" of the world's social structures and a "minority" of the world's cultures. This is not to deny the validity of those social and cultural experiences as regional or limited to certain groups of people. All we say here is that they are only a small part of the human experience.[15]

The problem is that North America, Western Europe and Japan command enormous resources which they use in the creation and advancement of knowledge both for the human sciences and the natural sciences. The United Nations through UNESCO has simply reflected this control of resources. When the Reagan administration was dissatisfied with the thrust of UNESCO under an African, the U.S. simply withheld its contribution to UNESCO until Mr. Bow and his multicultural policies were removed from the leadership of UNESCO.

With the control of these enormous resources by powerful governments, foundations and corporations, Japan, Canada and the United States together with the western European countries, simply support and reinforce scholarship that does not question centers and perspectives. The Eurocentric perspective replicates itself unchallenged in succeeding generations of scholars throughout the world. That is academic hegemony in practice.

5. Non-Hegemonic Europe Centered Perspective

The emergence of anticolonialist thinking even in Europe itself during this century, has given strength to a second and non-hegemonic type of the Europe centered intellectual enterprise which should not be confused with the totalizing hegemonic one we just discussed. The two often cover overlapping areas and become indistinguishable.

This second form of Europe centered perspective represents for European knowledge formation, the legitimate a priori self-positioning that scholars in all other regions of the world have to adopt in order to study social phenomena in this broad and complex global village in which we all live. In this context, Europe is as valid a point of departure as any other part of the world and a Europe centered perspective in this sense is a healthy and necessary framework for a conceptual base.

This Europe centered perspective would be non-imperial in its implications and emphasize the practical convenience of using the European observation center for researchers. The perspective would concede that other, equally legitimate centers of observation exist around the world such as the Africa centered or Asia centered. This non-hegemonic perspective would also stipulate that from these "diverse" centers around the world would come information that will eventually lay the only proper foundation on which to build a "pluriversal" perspective in history and the social sciences. However, this was also not the dominant Europe centered perspective in the past. The hegemonic perspective as we indicated earlier was more dominant.

But there are encouraging signs of a process of re-examination out of the contemporary intellectual crisis in history and the social sciences. William Appleman Williams provides us with an example of a prominent Europe centered historian who began to question the assumptions of Eurocentric theories of capitalism and Marxism regarding historical development. Why he came to question these assumptions is very important for the Africa centered perspective of history and for the advocates of a polycentered social science.

Williams was convinced by the early 1980s that the modern quest for the universal would lead to tragedy. He denounced modern ideas and modern institutions, Capitalist and Marxist alike, because their logic was endless growth. He maintained that 'when capitalists and communists embraced time, they did so because they believed they could control the future and time for them was not unpredictable'.[16]

Williams believed that socially vibrant local commonwealths that were truly pluralistic could be constructed within history--to replace modern culture which was dying because of its ideological and institutional pretensions to the universal. He viewed the nation state in America and the Soviet Union as a major mechanism used by a prideful people in their attempt to impose their will on the diversity of human experience.

Williams came to admire the sense of community in the decentralized societies created by early Christians and by First Americans. He especially admired the First Americans for 'their sophisticated understanding of how to create and sustain a symbiotic relationship with the land--and how they evolved a sense (and the rituals) of time, place and pace that could have helped the majority of twentieth century Americans sustain their own traditions of community and common humanity during the process of urbanization and industrialization'. In all this he concedes the positive role that plural perspectives play and how they help a diverse society enrich its thinking and find humane solutions to people's problems.

Williams went even further and argued that history becomes tragedy whenever a person or a people claim that their position was eternally valid and that all other positions were in absolute error. Williams also raised an all important issue when he asked:

> Can one hope for participation in economic, political, and social life, for the experience of community, unless one accepts boundaries and diversity?[17]

Thus Williams came to admire the positive social energy that emerges from the contributions of multiple centers.

The African American scholar Harold Cruse first posed this possibility of multiculturism in America in his Crisis of the Negro Intellectual in 1967 and finally fleshed out his ideas more clearly in Plural but Equal in 1987. Cruse, I should point out, does not directly advocate an Africa centered perspective. Yet, in so many words, the logic of his arguments points to the necessity of an America that is a social habitat for a culturally plural but equal peoples. He argues that the very foundation of the United States harbored the seeds of multiple cultures from America, Europe and Africa. Of Africa's impact he argues that "American Civilization, as we know it could not have been built without African slavery [enslavement?]" and that America's Founding Fathers' intent to create an `all white [European American] nation' from the outset was rendered impossible by the "presence of considerable numbers of Africans in the colonies (plus the presence of aborigines [First Americans])". Therefore America was, from the start, a salad bowl of Africans, Europeans and First Americans that could realistically aspire, at best, to become a welded pot for all its people but could never be a true and unqualified melting pot. For purposes of our argument here, the intellectual acceptance of cultural diversity which is at the heart of an ongoing model of `America's becoming' allows Europe centered, Africa centered, Asia centered and America centered perspectives to coexist in creative intercourse in a manner automatically denied by claims of universalism in hegemonic Europe centered theories.[18]

There is yet a general attack on 'historical culture' by Sande Cohen which also directs us to the need for a many centered perspective. Cohen maintains, in rather cumbersome phraseology, that "historical thought is a manifestation of reactive thinking--about, which blocks the act of thinking-to." "History," this critic from the field of communication argues, is not relevant to critical thinking "because what actually occurs by means of 'historical thought' is the destruction of a fully semanticized present." This well meant critique, confuses the consequences of a Europe centered hegemonic perspective with the study of history in general. For example, the writer's objection to the "intellectual acceptance of academia as a just player in the overall organization of knowledge," mirrors the doubts expressed by such diverse thinkers as Williams, Lukacs, Asante, Karenga and Bernal who would certainly agree that "academia is not [merely] a reactive subjectivity whose writings result in paradigms that objectify reality [but] . . . that academic writing is immersed in the creation of reactive thinking . . . and . . . academic historical texts release their built-in intellectual and cultural effects, . . . [which are then] consumed by readers who . . . become "renters and not owners of their own know-how."[19]

This criticism within context may apply especially to the hegemonic aspect of the Europe centered perspective we discussed earlier. However there are built-in problems in Cohen's criticism. First, relatively few people are usually engaged in the writing of the history read by the many. The major question, it seems to me, should center around whether the history that is written liberates the minds of the many and also empowers them by encouraging them to think in ways that center their observations about themselves on their own historical roots. Some frameworks imprison the perspectives of ordinary people by encouraging them to view themselves solely through perspectives of outsiders who may bear hostile or indifferent attitudes to communities.

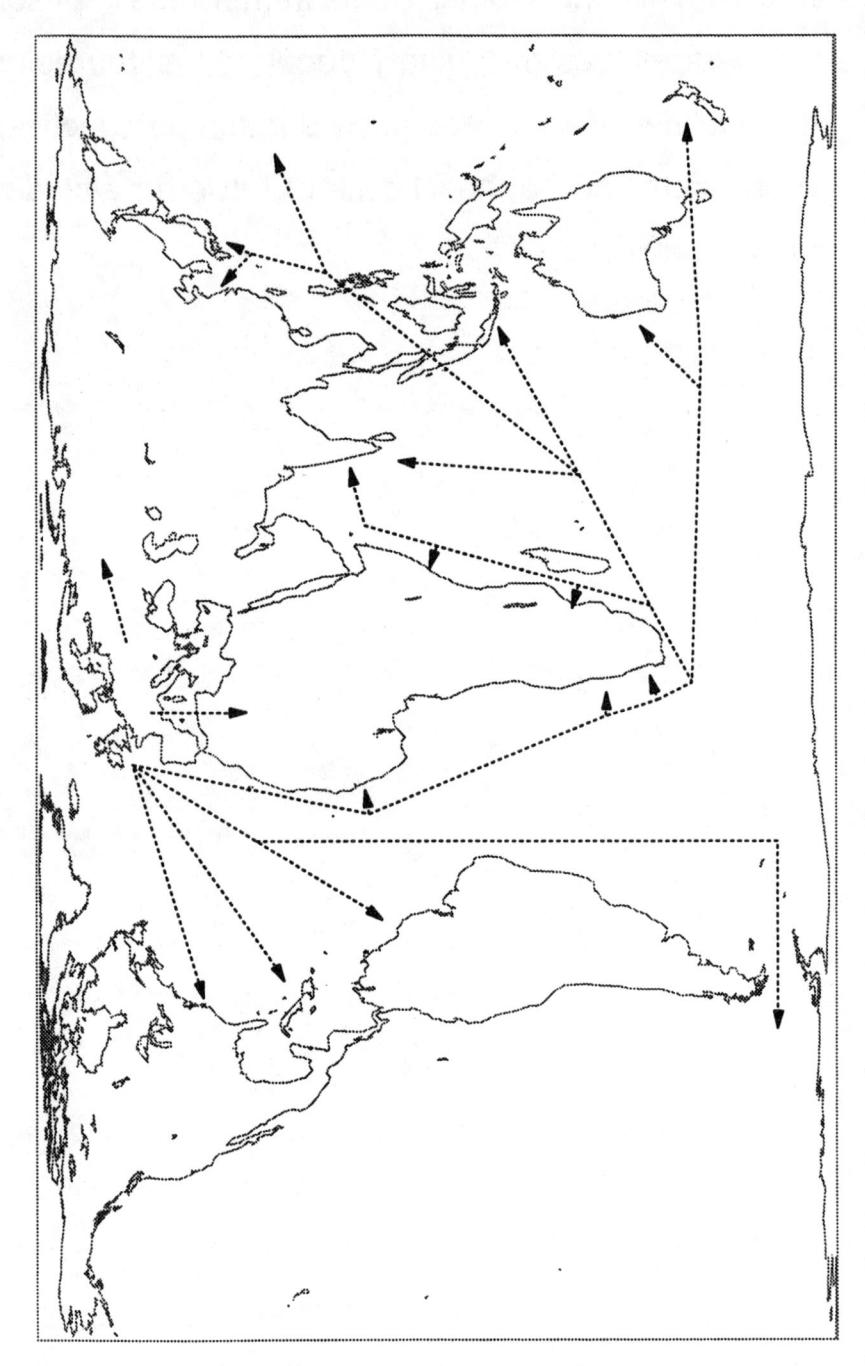

64 An Introduction to The Africa Centered Perspective of History

Europe Centered Historical Movement

6. The Africa Centered Perspective and Gender

The Africa centered perspective of history revolves around the simple argument that the African historical experience can rightfully provide a focus for scholarship that explains the world and its developments through the prism of African eyes and experience, and, given the past negative experience with hegemonic Europe centered scholarship, can provide an affirmative focus for African people. That focus however should not be based on the need to submerge or deny the validity of the perspectives of other people in this world just because they happen not to be African. In this context, the Africa centered perspective will also make a major contribution by advocating for tolerance and inclusion in a multicultural world people from different regions of the world have a right to declare and to affirm their perspective in creating and developing independent intellectual perspectives from which a global, "pluriversal" and multicentered perspective will emerge and influence the human sciences of the next century.

The world of Africans and descendants of Africans and the world of scholarship about them is still the only one at the end of the Twentieth Century that retains a 'colonial' signature whereby experts and authorities outside African communities control knowledge creation and exceed experts inside those communities. This does not apply to Europe, Asia or the Americas. This has led to an unfortunate predilection among Africans to concede expert knowledge to outsiders. African people have tended in the past to surrender the right to academic self affirmation to others, thereby accepting conclusions of a Eurocentric framework that have assigned a permanent peripheral role to the Africa centered perspective in the world's growing knowledge industry. Indeed, many of the 'authorities' who study and write about the African world and exercise great influence over the outside world's perception of Africa and Africans, the understanding of its value priorities, the vision of its future and the capacity to define its very essence for insiders and outsiders alike, often are not burdened with the knowledge of single African or African derived language.

There is another special reason for an African centered perspective at the end of the Twentieth Century. The use of an Africa centered framework provides an opportunity to contribute corrective historical insights in the analysis of the world's social phenomena because of the unique relationship of the African continent to the emergence of homo sapiens and the subsequent rise of human cultures.

Male-Female Relationships

Further, if an Africa centered perspective draws its inspiration from the instructive anvil of early history, it should be imbued with sensitivity towards the complementary gender roles of men and women for continuing the biological and cultural security and survival of the community. Gender complementarity rather than competition (however inadequate its fairness to women at different historical times, as judged in the context of Twentieth Century consciousness), was and still is as imperative to African cultural survival in the word of today as it is still critical to continuing the biological survival and security of all Africans into the future.[20]

There are radical implications for historical research and value formation that flow from recognizing the centrality of gender complementarity. For example, the very nature of the early recorded division of labor by gender which assigned to women the task of gathering vegetable products close to "home" while men hunted animals (mobile protein) further afield, strongly supports the contention that the domestication of plants or the famed neolithic revolution that led to agriculture, was the invention of women rather than men. If this were indeed the case in the early history of Africa, the dominance of women in the sector of agricultural production in the African experience is more in keeping with their "traditional" role than the theories of Europe centered developmentalist scholars of the 1960s who assumed that male dominated agriculture should automatically be the model for Africa.

There is also another fundamental issue that relates to the historical distinction between the individual rights of women and the group rights of women in specific African societies. These historical group rights which assured women collective power, economic leverage and social control over important public affairs were replaced by the "property" concept and then by the bestowal of "equal" individual rights with men before and during the colonial period and independence periods. Ironically, this development led to the loss of effective group control of aspects of public life by African females in exchange for highly publicized tokenist gestures to individual women accompanied by substantive peripheralization of women as a group in public and economic affairs. The colonial and post-colonial realignment of gender rights did not, in terms of power, restore the precolonial group leverage that women exercised in many African societies. Instead of expanding the sphere of effective group rights that women already enjoyed onto the terrain of individual rights, women were granted individual rights that lacked an internal material resource base to sustain them. The process of sorting all this out continues as Africa and African people outside Africa struggle to redefine themselves and gender roles in a post-industrial world.

The relations of men and women are tied to group rights and status rights of men and women in the overall power alignment in society. These relations in turn are anchored on deeply held values that affect the collective welfare of a society. Individual rights are tied to family and community and do not stand by themselves as they do in Western formulations of women's rights. A man and a woman are part of a family and a community and the relations of a man and woman will reflect and reinforce the welfare of the community. A balance between individual rights and societal obligations echoes the phrase that Abu Abarry is fond of saying: "I am because we are."

Hegemony

The lure of hegemony is not only a temptation to Europe centered scholarship. The Afrocentric perspective can also carry hegemonic undertones when all claims to progress in all regions of the world are explained in terms of the African presence and the African presence alone. This hegemonic tendency, though ego-boosting to people whose egos have been historically bruised by Eurocentric racism and prejudice should be vehemently rejected by Africa centered scholars for two reasons. First, a hegemonic approach automatically renders other peoples of the world historically invisible and/or as a "dehumanized" entity. This by any other name is always wrong. When others have to be demeaned in order to celebrate the importance of one's perspective or one's culture the relentless journey to justify oppression and distortion through spurious reasoning has already began. This anti-human tendency also sets in motion a counter active tendency among those people which it seeks to dehumanize, leading to challenge and confrontation. A hegemonic tendency becomes unnecessary if we view the Africa centered perspective as a part of a global intellectual movement of liberation and a step towards the creation of a "pluriversal" and diversity affirming perspective in the human sciences of the Twenty First Century.

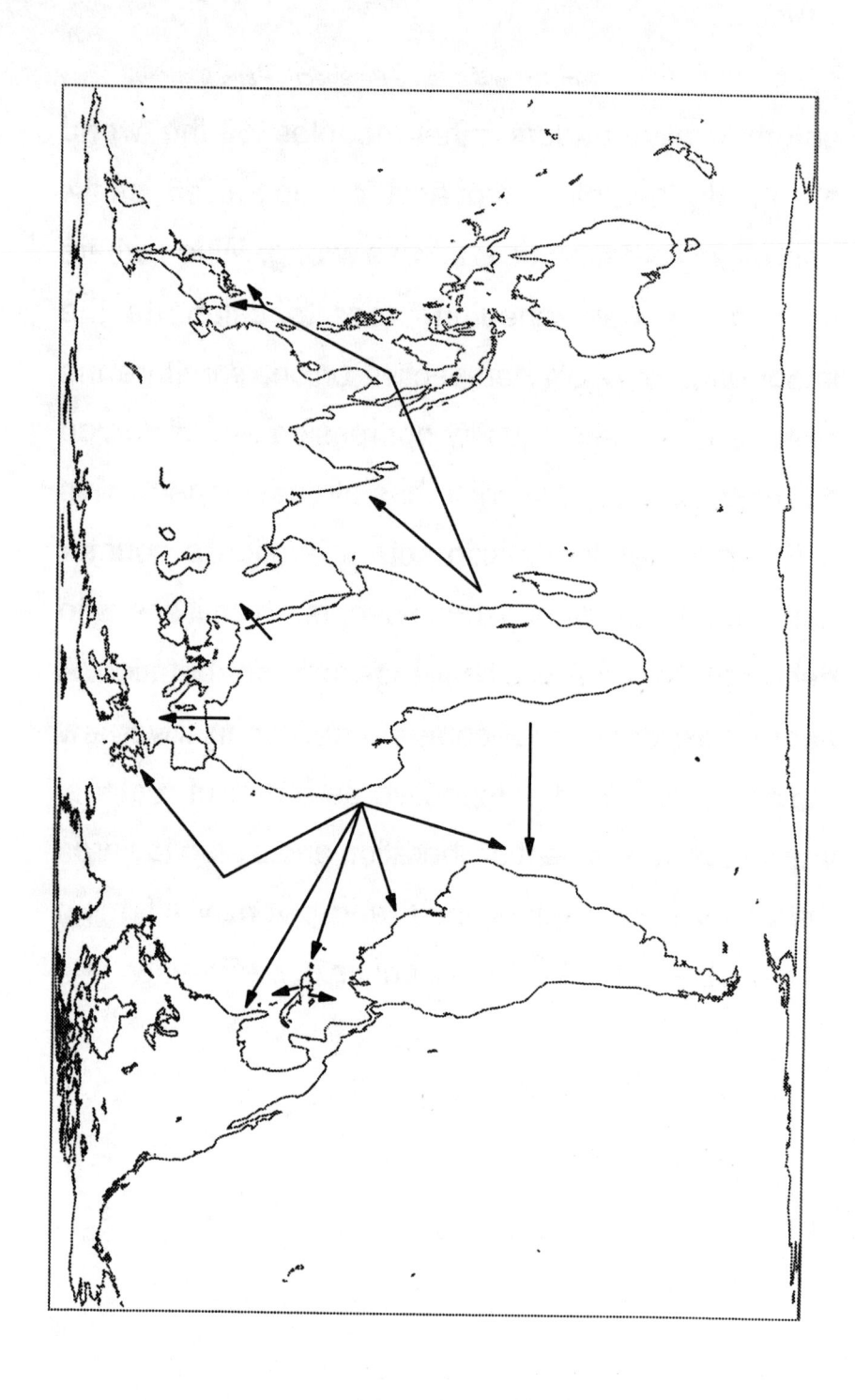

Africa Centered Historical Movement

Part II. Applying The Africa Centered Perspective

A. Concept Building

We create concepts, the baskets of our knowledge, based on our particular center and its perspective. An excellent example is the word "civilization" and its opposite "barbarian." Members of a culture see themselves as civilized and outsiders as "strange," exotic and "uncivilized." It is natural for a people to center the events of the world with themselves as the "center" of developments. These various "centered" perspectives have to interact and create a transcendent form of viewing the world. This is why a "multicentered" perspective may be the goal for the next century. Intellectual tragedy occurs when people assumes concepts and perspectives from a different center and internalize these concepts. The result is unconscious self-deprecating analysis and conceptual confusion.

The concept of Third World and the implications of Marxist theory will be used as examples of location displacement and intellectual obfuscation.

7. The Concept of the Third World

The practice of regarding the majority of the world's people as the "Third World" began innocently as a positive and affirmative act at a conference in Bandung in 1955. Leaders of African and Asian countries who did not view themselves and their countries as ideological appendages of either the Communist East or Capitalist West, defined themselves as a "Third Force" in world affairs. They insisted that they were perfectly capable of judging international developments on their own merits from their own independent perspective.

In the social turmoil of the liberation struggles of the 1960s in America, the concept of "Third World peoples" further assumed a positive connotation of struggling oppressed "outsiders" when students from the African American, Asian American, Hispanic American and Native American communities banded together to defend their interests in newly desegregated European American institutions of higher education.

Economic developmentalist scholars in the 1960s

and 1970s turned the term "Third World" into a dependent concept predicated on poverty, low economic performance, low per capita income and unfavorable health statistics. Third World and Fourth World under United Nations designation have now come to signify human poverty, lack of human skills and natural resources for self-generating economic development. The terms in fact describe a peripheral relationship of dependence and imply the status of supplicant states who are perennial beggars. This has also generated an emerging academic industry of Third World Studies outside the "Third World." This new academic thrust covers topics ranging from the history of development to investment policies for development, from economics to policy studies.

Whatever the merits of the earlier use of the term "Third World," the dependent concept that is now sweeping academia has become problematic in itself for several reasons. First it is a peripheralizing concept which focuses the definition of parts of the world on their economic subservience to the `Industrial' countries. It smothers the positive affirmation of the people in culturally diverse regions of the world.

Second, it oversimplifies by placing over 80% of the world's people on one side as a counterpoint to 20% of the world's people who live in industrialized countries. The peoples of Asia, Africa and Latin America are lumped together as if they can be fruitfully studied through generalized concepts from a revived "colonial scholarship" which substitutes development studies for the old reliable stand-by, "colonial anthropology." Many institutions of higher learning in the developed countries believe that <u>one</u> specialist can cover everything from sociology, anthropology, literature, politics, economics and history about all of Africa, Latin American and Asia, while six to eight specialists are necessary to study one century of "history" for North America or Europe alone. The change of terminology to international studies does not alter this basic built-in conceptual distortion.

Finally, the logic of three or four worlds has outlived its usefulness and makes little sense in the post Cold War world of Yeltsin, Walesa and Deng Xioping. The dependency focus that is so dear to the crusade for social justice, that neo-Marxist and neo-liberal theorists espouse, may be well meant but it appears to have deteriorated into a benign form of Europe centered hegemony that peripheralizes the many of the world in reference to the few.

As an example Pierre Joulee is critical of the expression "Third World" which he describes as the "backyard of imperialism" that conceals the reality of imperial relations while serving objectively, "to cause confusion." However he divided the world into socialist and capitalist camps before the demise of the Communist camp. Paul Bairoch employed "Third World" synonymously with "less developed," "developing," "underdeveloped," and "non-industrialized." "Developed" is defined solely in the economic sense. J. E. Goldthorpe was more explicit. He wrote "[if] . . . the affluent industrial countries of the modern world are grouped into those of the "West" and "East," capitalist and communist, then the poor countries constitute a "Third World" whose small command over resources distinguishes them from both." The problem with this type of rather simplistic classification is that if these countries eliminate their poverty, they have to be fitted into either the `capitalist' or `communist' pigeon hole and the Communist pigeon hole no longer exists.[21]

The collapse of Communism in Eastern Europe and Russia in the 1990s demonstrated the dependency status of concept which described the rest of the world in terms of European developments. So-called Afrocommunism became "parentless" without the former "Eastern bloc countries." How did this come about? We will understand this development when we discuss Marxist theory next.

8. Marxist Theory and an Africa Centered perspective

The theories of Karl Marx, Lenin and Mao Tse Tung have relevance in discussing the merits of an Africa centered perspective. Marxist theory has an analytic aspect that can interact with an Africa centered perspective of history. Marxist theory also has a predictive aspect that is in direct conflict with an Africa centered approach. I have minor disagreements with Marxist theory as an analytical tool and as a critique of domination. Under specific conditions, this theory can and does coexist and enrich the methodological repertoire of scholars who espouse an Africa centered perspective of history.

However the elements of Marxist theory that claim to predict future developments in human affairs through a special insight into the "universal laws" of social change, profoundly is incompatible with an Africa centered perspective as I understand it and as I have outlined it in the pages of this publication. What is even more disturbing is that when Marxist and neo-Marxist theoreticians claim "unqualified universalism" for the conceptual derivations from their metatheory of history which are based largely on the study of the European experience, they are simply extending, under the guise of a "radical program" and dimension, the application of a hegemonic Europe centered perspective. Therefore in its dogmatic form, the Marxist approach is antithetical to an Africa centered perspective. However when Marxist and neo-Marxist theory provides a significant social critique of the class conflicts and other economic and social factors associated with the social organization for production that accompanies the development and maturation process of merchant and industrial capitalism that began in Europe, insights from such historical critiques of society are helpful for analyzing social change terrain as areas of the world occupied by Africans become affected by the process of industrialization and urbanization under capitalism. It is, for example, appropriate to examine the relationship between public policy and the class interests of those who formulate it. It is equally appropriate to examine, through the prism of class and race, the issue of social access to publicly held resources by states.

The ultimate intellectual response by people who study developments from an Africa centered perspective will depend on how they analyze specific historical experiences and cultural value preferences that dictate for a community, where "acceptable social trade-offs" can be made and how a society defines such "acceptable social trade-offs." Like capitalist theory, when socialist theory is fitted to, and modified by, a people's culture, the theory ceases to be a mechanism of control by intellectuals over the minds of the masses and a restriction of workers' choice of options by upper class theoreticians. The modified or "praxified" theory becomes part of the dynamic tools for change that empowers workers and peasants to create and recreate their own culture of work. There seems to be the stirrings of such research applications for Marxist theory.[22]

The ultimate challenge we face in an Africa centered perspective is how to bring about changes that enhance social justice or Maat. This quest for social justice, as a driving force in people's affairs and

in societies committed to liberation, is not a monopoly of Marxists, neo-Marxists, and socialists. Other ideologies claim their right to the same objective through concepts such as democratization and co-determination. Different peoples and cultures inside and outside the parameters of what we can call the African world have addressed this issue. Some have met with a degree of measurable success in resolving problems surrounding interpersonal relationships or creating
social buffers of compromise that allow difficult social relations to work until proper solutions are found. Many of these same social practices have taken years of African experimentation through trial and error before they were successful. Some attempts have proven effective while others have failed.

One disturbing trend in the world African centered scholars should be keenly aware of is the tendency by technocrats and bureaucrats to resort to social engineering and when that fails to manipulate people's perception of social reality by issuing "deceptive information." This tendency is not only to be found among repressive regimes, but is often justified by progressive governments in the search of quick fix solutions to stubborn social problems. Victories on paper might dazzle audiences for a brief period. In the long term these fake "victories" usually prove to be inconsequential. In Eastern Europe the major flows of a system insensitive to its constituents finally buried the inefficient bureaucrats with their deceptive press reports of success. Victories that count in the long run are those whose principles are successfully ingrained into the cultural fabric of the lives of ordinary people-- a process that sometimes takes an inordinately long time to accomplish.

In the case of the African world, social changes that will last will be these that reflect an Africa centered perspective. As for ideologies, that do not effectively Africanize their value assumptions tend to enjoy a brief life span in the African, African American, African European, and African Asian cultural world.[21] Africans themselves have created ideologies which place African interests at the center. In such cases, time itself works for the centered focus.[23]

B. Historical Studies

An Africa centered perspective must be (1) gender sensitive in its approach because gender complementarity is necessary in society, and (2) its scope must be informed by a non-hegemonic premise. This means that an Africa centered perspective is aware of, and accepts other cultural-regional perspectives as equally valid. This perspective asserts that a multiplicity of centers enrich our understanding of cultural diversity as it reinforces our respect for the innovativeness of the peoples of the "world communities" in which we live. Two regions of the world provide excellent examples.

The United States of America and the Republic of South Africa are fertile fields for the application of an Africa centered perspective of history. Why? For a reason we have to retreat back into the respective past of these two countries. In the last millennium, people have moved, unevenly, from certain parts of the world to other parts. I call this uneven social phenomenon the creation of the "global pluriverse." Certain parts of the globe were touched lightly by this development and remained relatively homogeneous culturally and biologically as has been the case with Japan. We can call these parts of the world region A. Other areas experienced significant emigration and relatively modest immigration. This was the experience of western Africa and western Europe excluding the Iberian peninsula. We can regard these parts as region B. Other areas witnessed significant in-migration and modest levels of out-migration as was the case in the Americas and southern Africa. We can label these parts as region C. Within this context, these region C areas are the "confluence zones" where people from different continents and cultures met and interacted even under "imperial relations and hegemonic social structures" controlled by one group.

In the case of the area that was to become the United States of America, the original peoples, the First Americans, interacted with Europeans and with Africans. Later, before people from Asia and the Pacific rim joined in the confluence within a new political entity called the United States. In southern Africa, the indigenous Africans interacted with the incoming Europeans and Asians. In both cases, control of land and resources of the land gradually came under the control of the Europeans and the historical descriptions that emerged and became popular were woven around a hegemonic Eurocentric framework. An Africa centered perspective in both areas would highlight the struggle for independence and the concern over social developments by the Africans who subscribed to a multicultural context of cultural difference without social hierarchy.

I could probably make an equally strong case for using Brazil and Kenya, Algeria and Jamaica or Puerto Rico and Zimbabwe. Ultimately, I selected the United States and South Africa because I am more familiar with historical developments in the two countries and because a great deal has been written about both countries although the available information has not always been even. The conclusion I draw from these two countries can be extended with appropriate modifications to other comparable areas.

A significant historical field for my purpose

therefore is the African diaspora in the land area that has become the United States of America. The other significant field for comparative purposes is the southern part of the ancestral continent in the land area now known as South Africa (also known as Azania to some of its inhabitants). Historical treatment of Africans and the descendants of Africa in these two areas teaches us valuable lessons about cultural coexistences hegemonic and non-hegemonic Europe centered perspectives and the contrasting Africa centered perspective. The treatment of these two areas of contemporary concern for the Africa centered perspective of history will be relatively brief and suggestive in this publication. Brief treatment here suggests a mountain of academic work that awaits the next generation of enterprising scholars who are willing to pursue an intellectual path that combines technical expertise in historical methodology with an affirmation of an Africa centered universe of discourse as a central part of the research paradigm.

The position I adopt in this discussion concerning the African historical record follows the framework outlined by Cheikh Anta Diop. I establish Ancient Kemet [Egypt] as the classical reference point for the discussion of African history. Drawing from pre-dynastic and dynastic ideas of African religion, government, medicine, architecture and agriculture, later developments and social accomplishments among people of African descent are analyzed in an interconnected temporal context rather than on the basis of an extreme diffusionist model. I firmly believe that an Africa centered perspective of history cannot be sustained as a systematic field of study without its connection to the ancient African cultures of the Nile valley. Without reference to Kemet, African history is indeed, in the words of Cheikh Anta Diop, an enterprise "suspended in mid-air." We can speculate that ancient Kemet either provides the origin or shares in an original African culture now unknown which was located to the South or West. The sectionalist focus on subsaharan or tropical Africa, ignores the cultural interaction in Africa before the desiccation of the Sahel in historical time and the advent of Islam in the seventh century of the Current Era.

9. African American History

My first concern here will be to demonstrate the consequences of employing an Africa centered perspective in reconstructing the history of African-Americans.

As I indicated earlier, we should always distinguish between (1) history as the totality of all past events among people and (2) history as the reconstructed or recalled record by scholars, griots and other specialists. History in the second sense is then transmitted to the minds of a new generation as collective memory and the process repeats itself for every generation. This is the history that can be manipulated to distort collective consciousness or fail to be transmitted to the next generation altogether. The example of the modern Egyptians is instructive. By 1800 the people of Egypt knew little or nothing about the accomplishments of their forebears four thousand years earlier. They did not even know how to transcribe Medu Netcher (the hieroglyphs) around them on stone. It took European scholars and the "Rosetta Stone" to unravel the mystery of the pyramids built by the Egyptians themselves. Cultural genocide had been that complete and all-embracing since the time of the Persians. Even today, there are no guarantees except the work of a committed and conscientious community of scholars of "public memory" (historians) that what happens in the 1980s will be comprehensively and accurately understood in the 2080s. The preservation of an accurate account about what happens today is always at risk in the future.

An African American friend described a situation where an African-American parent vehemently denied that there was any connection between her family and Africa because her relatives came from the West Indies. In her mid-thirties, the parent learned for the first time that West Indians who looked liked her originally came from Africa. This may be an extreme example of the intellectual tragedy of temporal illiteracy and the continuing miseducation of African Americans. However, this tragedy is not a new phenomenon, it was noted by the prominent African American pioneer historian Carter G. Woodson five decades ago in the

Miseducation of the Negro. The need for African American historical and cultural connectedness for the sanity of African Americans has been argued most forcibly by Asante in The Afrocentric Idea (1987).[24]

The trade in physically enslaved Africans was one of the historically significant ways that changed the biological and cultural composition of populations in Africa and the Americas. (This trade is conventionally referred to as the "slave trade.") The term slave and slave trade may appear neutral but from an Africa centered perspective, they harbor an implicit element of submission to enslavement by Africans and acceptance of the condition by African Americans. According to approaches that peripheralize African experience, these African and their African American progeny supposedly begin to "resist" and "rebel" against their condition of enslavement only after someone outside their cultural community informed them of their rights as human beings. Once these people who knew nothing about freedom and human rights were properly motivated by these "seditious" ideas, they became unmanageable for a while as they resorted to riots, conspiracies and revolts. According to this scenario, they have no "culture or vision of freedom" of their own. Furthermore, "order" was restored by lawful authorities who "put down" the rebellion despite the terrible misgiving in the consciences of some of these authorities about this unfortunate institution that enslaved Africans and African Americans known euphemistically in the literature of the time as the "peculiar" institution. In the narratives, some victimizers are transformed into saviors of "law and order" while the struggling victims become "fanatics" and "insurgents" but never "freedom fighters."

But we turn the historical picture around when we employ an Africa centered perspective. First this perspective compels us to distinguish between the focus on African Americans in American history which centers on individual accomplishment without reference to African Americans as a collective group, and the history of African Americans which centers on the group. It is possible to document progress employing the first focus without significant social improvements according to the second focus. Each of the two foci can be used and yield valid insights. However the implications of those results differ and should not be confused when we assess the status of African Americans, as a group, at any point in the unfolding drama that was America.

With the Africa centered focus, we also recognize in principle and at the outset, the rights of the enslaved Africans and African Americans to freedom, as a people equally endowed by their Creator with the same <u>inalienable rights</u> "of life, liberty and the pursuit of happiness." There is no need to equivocate concerning the "historical sentiments of the time" in regard to African enslavement. Such equivocations belong to the hegemonic Europe centered perspective of the status of Africans and African Americans in continental North America. If we agree that from our chosen center and its perspective, the enslaved Africans possessed these primary rights to begin with, then, when they seek to assert their God-given rights for themselves, for their children and for their parents, we can conceptualize the struggle of the Africans and African Americans [and here I am purposely telescoping the historical narrative for effect], as trying to restore in the new land (America), a just social order or what the ancient Africans on the Nile called ma'at (social justice), where the Africans found a distorted, unjust and dehumanizing social order. By refusing to go along with their enslavement even when the prospect of immediate personal freedom appeared unattainable, first the Africans, and, later the African Americans, established an important moral victory in world history and became an historical example of human tenacity and love of freedom for all people engaged in the struggle for liberation around the world.[25]

This way these historical Africans represented more than a minor local "problem" to be solved by those who continued their enslavement. They represented a historic challenge just as African Americans are a continuing litmus test for the very essence of American democracy. The African American experience was not the first nor was it to be the last time that the fight for human freedom by the sons and daughters of Africa was reduced in historical stature to a side show even when as in eighteenth-century Haiti their fate was at the center of the major human question of the day. Historians employing the Africa centered perspective can restore the balance in the narratives of world history. No one else will be as consistently committed as the Africa centered scholar in documenting and reconstructing this aspect of the global human struggle against injustice and dehumanization.

However, another very disturbing consequence of the hegemonic Europe centered perspective, is the way the trade in enslaved Africans has been described in most history textbooks. American history books tend to celebrate a miraculous social transformation of Africans in the middle of the Atlantic ocean. In an ocean that was once known as the Ethiopian Sea in the sixteenth century, the Africans commit physical and cultural genocide by <u>disappearing without a trace</u>. They either complete a process that reformulates them into "Negroes" on the coasts of West and West Central Africa or undergo a rapid social metamorphosis to this status at sea. Once the Africans had transformed themselves into slaves, negroes, Negroes and Blacks, they were now ready to play their ascribed <u>peripheral</u>

roles as social adjuncts to the Europe centered enterprise whose glorious narrative swept across the histories of the Americas using the grand concepts of liberty, human freedom and the American dream. Only the First Americans occupy a worse role conceptually since they are relegated to being the creators of a "wilderness" that had to be tamed by European Americans to build the "City on the Hill" which becomes a shining beacon of human liberty. The "negroes and the slaves" provide labor to the European American colonists for a few hundred years before transforming themselves once more into a massive social problem associated with crime, gambling, substance abuse and family disintegration in the twentieth century.[26]

In this historical scenario, the ultimate reality for African Americans is that they become a social problem for someone else to solve. And they rely on help and on assistance from outside their community and outside the culture they created. Some writers even suggest that the culture of African Americans has become so "deficient" that the children should be taken from their families and nurtured by the military or by middle class white families. Only this way can they be truly assimilated into the American "mainstream" and stand any chance of a productive human existence. Their African-American culture has no positive attributes of any kind except those aesthetic gifts that qualify them to become great entertainers or the physical prowess that fits them to be the gladiators of modern sports. Since their future lies in becoming "like the mainstream" politically, economically and especially culturally, the major goal in studying African-Americans is to identify suitable policies that can move them from their current "abnormal status" and help them to lose all cultural vestiges of their unfortunate cultural heritage and assimilate into the "mainstream."[27]

The double standard [and contradictory premise] represented by this approach quickly becomes obvious when the same scholars rightfully celebrate the contributions of such richly diverse communities as the Irish-Americans, German-American, Greek-American, Jewish-American, Polish-American, Asian-American and Italian-American in the making of America's cultural and social quilt. African Americans are denied this sense of contribution to the formation of America's historical community. Scholars of African-American history who attempt to deny the presence of Africans in historical North America encourage the myth of Black origins in Mississippi, South Carolina, Maryland, Alabama, Florida and the West Indies. An Africa centered perspective views these areas as legitimate incubation centers for the reformulation of a neo-African culture as an African-American culture and consciousness on American soil. Denial of a connection to previous African culture is a form of cultural genocide that affirms the aquatic Maafa of the "middle passage." African Americans lose the historical relevance of this "holocaust" since those women and men were tossed to the sharks; revolted on ships and committed suicide rather endure enslavement, were not kinfolk from the Carolinas and Georgia. A truncated version of the historical roots of African Americans leaves African Americans, as a people among other peoples in America, suspended in their social and cultural origins as 'products of plantations'. Such a historical perception easily leads to self hatred.[28]

An Africa centered approach to the history of the Americans from Africa interfaces with the long history of Africa and then demonstrates how within historical time, the trade in enslaved Africans primarily affected Africa by the random removal of people of all social classes and that it represented the second wave of West Africans (Post Columbus as opposed to Pre-Columbus) to come to the Americas. Certainly, the ships that loaded enslaved Africans in the ports of Whydah, Lagos and Cape Coast, unloaded enslaved Africans in Barbados, Kingston, Charleston, Baltimore, Jamestown, Philadelphia, New York, and Salem. The name "Guinea towns" used to describe settlements of Africans and African Americans in colonial and revolutionary America clearly recognized the African origins of their inhabitants.

The Stono revolt of 1739 in South Carolina is a significant example of an African revolutionary initiative. Africans from Angola decided to free themselves from their enslavement and to use the medium of the drum to communicate with others. South Carolina's pro-enslavement authorities banned drums after this revolt because the drums represented an African form of communication that the class of enslavers could not control or understand in a colony whose recorded majority was made up of enslaved Africans at the time of the American Revolution. The irony of the American Revolution in the specific case of South Carolina was that it represented a political victory for that class of Americans from Europe who violated the human rights of Africans. The victory continued the enslavement of the African American majority in the State as well as the peripheralization and dispossession of the native American indigenes.[29]

What is always critical to document when we employ an Africa centered perspective in the writing of African American history is to unravel the secrets of population composition of the peoples of African descent who lived in North America during the formative 1700s. If, as we generally suggest, close to half of them were African-born, they were unquestionably Africans. During the last decade of the eighteenth century and the first two decades of the nineteenth century, we witness the historic emergence of an African American creole population, a collective self-made people, combining elements of African, First American and European heritages into a unique Africa centered cultural synthesis fashioned out of the experience of their lives on the American continent.

Once we recognize that the first "Black" Alabamians, South Carolinians, Virginians, Floridians, Pennsylvanians and Marylanders were Africans, then myths and delusions disappear and scholars come to terms with the utility of an Africa centered historical perspective that incorporates change among, and the creative contributions of, African Americans. We then recognize that the major deficiency of American history as currently taught is not that it places European Americans at the center of developments but that it denies the equally significant roles of African Americans and First Americans at the core of the early history and cultural formation of the American social experiment. An Africa centered perspective of America does not deny the process of a becoming America which involves many peoples and many cultures. It opposes the silencing of the historical African voice in the story.[30]

The Africa centered perspective also creates a new focus for evaluating the historical choices of the immigrant Africans and of the African Americans in their actions and endeavors. The greatest challenge facing this perspective is the process of explicating an evolving African-American hierarchy of historical values that would undergird explanations of choices made by the immigrant Africans in North America and later by a communally self made people, the African Americans. The reconstruction and application of an historical cultural framework of Africa centered values still requires painstaking research and compilation--but it is there in the historical record to be extrapolated and analyzed by researchers. It holds the key to attitudes towards other cultures, other races and other ethnic groups in a new environment and a new land. Whether some African Americans abandoned their core values and cultural reference in favor of different ones, whether some retained their value-reference more or less intact or whether others blended diverse heritages with that of others to create a novel social and cultural dynamic with new results are questions that will provide the basis for an ongoing and exciting research enterprise well into the distant future.

Africa Centered Focus and Contributionism

An Africa centered focus also encourages scholars to move away from uncritical "contributionism" where everything that "Blacks" did was the result of their Blackness and is proudly enumerated during annual celebrations. The Africa centered approach is not merely an outward form of glorifying pigmentology cast in academic guise. Scholars have to review and critique actions and accomplishments using a consistent yardstick that evaluates how those actions contributed to the liberation of the person and the enhancement of the lives of African Americans, other communities that have endured past dehumanization and all people. African Americans have to make the world safe for the fulfillment of the person according to the values they cherish. Actions and contributions should also be evaluated for their consistency with an Africa centered hierarchy of historical values that places high priority on the worth of the person. Scholars who employ this

Africa centered perspective have to rethink the significance of the "Buffalo" soldiers. They have to ask themselves tough questions such as: whether a humanistic hierarchy of values would rank as positive the destruction of First American villages and cultures or countenance the forceful expropriation of First American lands. An Africa centered perspective is not necessarily a blanket approval of, and justification for everything Africans or African-Americans do. It is a self-disciplining perspective; it creates a self affirming criterion of values and it embodies a practical concern for the positive welfare of Africans and all of humanity. African Americans should not study history in order to prove that they are human, that they are "intelligent," that they can invent, that they can sing opera or dance a minuet. These human abilities should be regarded as a given by scholars. Therefore, Africa centered scholars should be careful not to glorify African Americans simply because they could perform certain feats that European Americans did, or could build as the people of Europe built. To do so is to embrace an uncritical intellectual subservience to a Europe centered perspective and indirectly to prove the English dictum that "Imitation is the sincerest form of flattery."[31]

We can try to explain the impact of the Africa centered perspective on the history of African Americans by using the metaphor of a train and passengers. African Americans are like people on a station platform who have been trying to convince the conductor of Train America that they are entitled to a seat on the approaching train. As the train pulls into the station, they suddenly realize that the destination of the train is an equally proper issue to discuss with the conductor. If the destination suggests that the train is headed for a rendezvous with social disaster, the privilege of getting on board will offer only a short-term advantage. To be true to their fellow travellers, to themselves and to what they have learned from their own history, they have a duty to raise questions about the final destination of "train America."

10. South African History

It should be fairly simple to show the need for an Africa centered perspective in the study of the history of Africans on the ancestral continent. However, this is not so easy since the bulk of books written on the history of Africa reflect hegemonic and nonhegemonic Europe centered perspectives. Even major African scholars still write proudly about the "discovery" of their ancestors by European explorers without appreciating the intellectual implication of terms like "discover" when they are not qualified. This state of affairs is the prime result of Africans internalizing an hegemonic Europe centered perspective. Too many African and other well intended scholars of Africa are effectively imprisoned in a twilight zone of African peripheralization. This condition may be changing with the emergence of a new assertive generation of scholars. African universities which should become the academic nurseries of the re-emergence of this traditionally Africa centered intellectual flame even as they continue to open their doors to perspectives, methodologies and viewpoints from other parts of the world, unfortunately, continue to be bastions of a hegemonic Europe centered perspective and have effectively shut out any serious participation of Africa centered perspectives of research and scholarship.

Most literature on South African history is quintessentially Europe centered even when it is written by "radical" scholars. The basic premise of all analysis adopts a Europe centered perspective when it begins with the "discovery" of the Cape of Good Hope by the Portuguese in the fifteenth century. From this apparently innocuous premise and from the foundation of a Dutch Refreshment Station in 1652, every historical discussion and debate is centered. The records in Dutch, Portuguese, English, French and German dictate the breath and depth of South African history. From here it is a small step to identify the foundation of South Africa with the period between 1652 and 1795, and, to mark the beginning of education, religion, dance, theater, and mining with the actions of Europeans. The hegemonic Europe centered perspective controls everything before it, and apparently controls ling even the terms of debate about the post-apartheid South Africa of the future. In 1988 the revival of white liberalism in South Africa was highly touted in new books although this liberalism did not seem to make as significant a dent on voting South Africans of European descent as the conservative right parties in the elections. Liberals were described in the editorials of the Western press as the saviors of South Africa's future. This Europe centered vision is pervasive, and is so influential that even radical scholars argued about workers, laborers, and peasants as if these men and women were cultural "tabulae rasae" units within the "capitalistic" system without any independent cultural base or Africa centered premise of observation.[32]

In the context of South African history, an Africa centered perspective was further clouded by that great Europe centered experiment called apartheid in which European South Africans of Dutch descent imposed after they had appropriated the name derived from the African continent itself 'Afrikaner' for themselves. The minority government that the 'Afrikaners' controlled decreed terms of identity on Africans and other South

Africans. The minority government refused to call Africans. In turn African intellectuals and political leaders reacted by doing the most natural thing; they rejected the identity labels imposed on them and then embraced the Europe centered liberal alternative of "cosmopolitanism" which at least promised to give them back their dignity as human beings in the world. But this also confused their primary focus as Africans. The grandiose failure of apartheid after thirty years, opened the floodgates to the vision promised by Europe centered liberalism and radicalism. The Black Consciousness intellectuals and the Nationalist Wing within the Liberation Movement suspecting that something was amiss--advocated an independent intellectual affirmation for Africans and for Blacks--but were accused of a reverse form of racial chauvinism by Eurocentricists including the South African regime whose racist raison d'être had spawned more racially restricted laws than any other country since the heyday of Nazi Germany. The cultural chauvinism of a hegemonic Europe centered perspective continued to dominate the academic enterprise and to claim universality for a South African history and social science that essentially peripheralized the African majority.[33]

South Africa is different from the United States in very significant ways. The term South African in Europe centered literature refers to the country's <u>minority</u> inhabitants of European descent. When used without qualifications by Africa centered scholars, the term South African should refer to those Africans who live in the south of the African continent as unambiguously as the term West Africans connotes those Africans who live to the west of the African continent. When specific segments of the human inhabitants of the territorial area are discussed, then the term South African should be qualified appropriately. Those who identify themselves as South Africans should appreciate the implications of the emphasis on the second term in the phrase. That definition of South African is the only one consistent with an Africa centered perspective.

There are celebrated terms and popular usages in the Europe centered historiography of South Africa that need to be discussed and dismissed by scholars who use an Africa centered perspective. For example, the obsessive distinction between Khoisan-speaking Africans and Isintu-speaking Africans in the literature distorts the historical relation ship between the two groups of <u>Africans</u>. Social intermixture, change, and interaction over time have obliterated neat social distinctions. Likewise The use of the term "Amazulu" in the 1980s demonstrates the incongruity inherent in rigid perceptions of ethnic groups. The present name Izulu or its endearment equivalent inzula is applied to the social results of a series of social developments that began in the nineteenth century with the state formation activities of King Shaka ka Senzangakhona and his successors who expanded the name of a family clan to apply to an emerging polity; it continued with the selective commitment of Isizulu to writing by the American missionaries; it was affected by the imposition of a British controlled colonial state that sought to rationalize its control of Africans; and was aided by a Europe centered school system that sought to standardize the language and socialize African children to what was the vision of a British colony called Natal; over and above all this was a cross cutting and conscious effort by Africans to build a society that respected their basic culture as they became enmeshed in an expanding vision of community as industrialization, urbanization, and commercialization of Natal threatened to tear them off their cultural moorings.[34]

The eclectic collection of ideas by emerging Black and African leaders often confused their focus and perched them uncomfortably between a Europe centered and an Africa centered perspective. They could never buy the universality of the Europe centered perspective because they knew enough from their personal and cultural experience about the Africa centered perspective. Because there were no intellectual institutions in which they could clarify or reconcile this dichotomy, some quickly adopted an intellectual perspective based on Europe centered "liberal" and "radical" philosophies.

As a result of this historical situation, many South African scholars are most at risk of becoming narrowly Europe centered in the name of making themselves "universal." The new "liberal vision under white leadership" in literature and scholarship which Western countries are underwriting, will further confuse and confound the future of South Africa. Africans have to create a liberated future for themselves based on democratic values and belief in the worth of the person. A nonhegemonic Africa centered perspective would affirm the African core of South Africa's cultural values but also admit change that has been influenced by the input of South Africans of Asian descent, South Africans of European descent and South Africans of mixed parentage. The rich mixture and plural perspectives, Asia centered and Europe centered provide automatic brakes to hegemonic tendencies in South Africa's Africa centered perspective. An example of this phenomenon already exists in the toi-toi's cultural resurgence among the youth of diverse backgrounds during the struggles of the 1980s and in the growing interest of Afrikaners to learn African languages. These are faint signs of hope for a cultural transformation in South Africa's future.[35]

The history of South Africa can be interpreted

using any number of milestones. For the Africa centered scholar the milestones must relate to significant experiences of South Africa's people--and especially its majority. Terms such as precolonial and precapitalist must clarify whose experience they are based on. For example, we have used the date 1652 in describing an aspect of South African history. We should all understand that until 1700, only a very small portion of South Africa was affected by the Dutch presence. In fact until the third decade of the nineteenth century, most South Africans lived in independent African controlled polities. The southwestern corner of South Africa experienced European colonialism centuries before the rest of South Africa.[36]

Two regions of South Africa, the Southwest and "Natal" on the east coast witnessed the arrival of Asian immigrants who later played an important part in the politics and economics of the regions in which they settled. Yet there are parts of South Africa which the Asian presence barely touched. Food preparation, political strategy and cultural change often took different routes because of the unique human mix in each region. An Africa centered perspective allows us to analyze and explicate the consequences of these differential time and differential settlement patterns. Sources in African and Asian languages could supplement sources in European language to uncover new insights through the aggressive use of sophisticated methodologies of social history that have proved helpful elsewhere. However, without an Africa centered perspective of history, as part of the research ingredient, one cannot understand all the ramifications of South African history.[37]

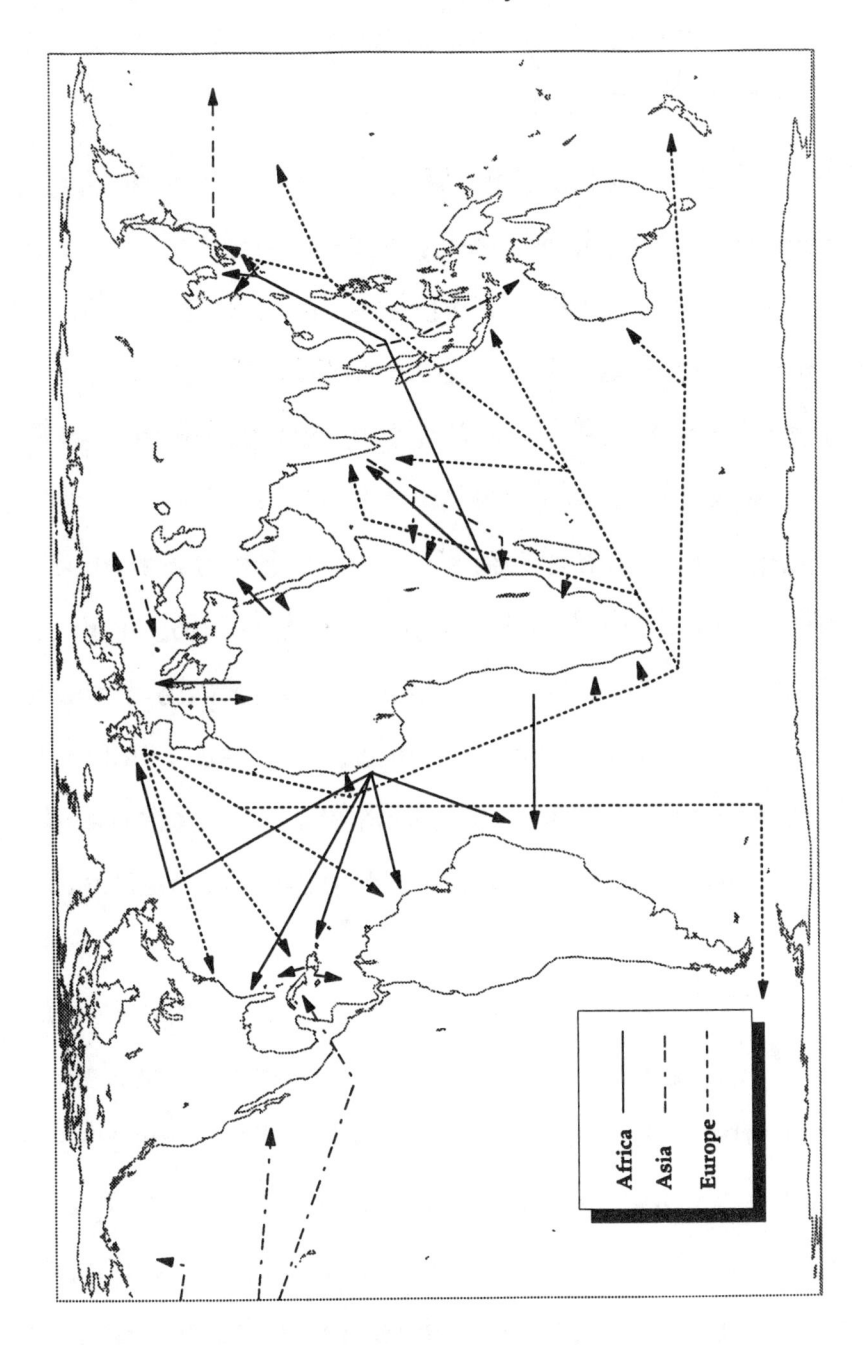

**Creation of the Global Pluriverse Since 2,000 B.P.
Since 2,000 B.P>**

11. Conclusion

Vigorous scholarly activity employing an Africa centered perspective must be supported and continued before the twenty first century arrives. African centered scholarship has begun to counter the element of self-peripheralization that had been internalized by African scholars trained in the European/Western tradition. Africa and descendants of Africans continue to be peripheralized by scholars who write about global developments. This view of Africa can only be changed by a major commitment by Africa centered scholars to a wider area of serious intellectual introspection and a reversal of the way Africa and its place in world history is viewed.[38]

The world stands at an important crossroads. The peoples of the world have to make decisions concerning the direction the global village will take in the twenty first century. The way we teach history and the social sciences to the youth of today will influence the attitudes of future leaders and scholars towards humanity in general and people around them in particular. The Africa centered perspective is a critical key that opens the gate to a non-hegemonic global human science. The perspective argues the case, not only for an Africa centered knowledge system, but also for the recognition of other regionally based perspectives that will place non-hegemonic Europe centered scholarship in its rightful context we can also recognize the contribution of perspectives to the world's pool of technical knowledge and their share in arousing interest in, and contributing to, the world's knowledge about people. Exposing the false premises of a hegemonic perspective will clear the way for a proper international appreciation of a non-hegemonic multicentered perspective in the human sciences.[39]

Given its predilection of creating theoretical models and artifices extrapolated from examples supplied by nature, the Africa centered perspective encourages a closer look at cyclical patterns in history, not in the mechanicistic sense alone but through a transcendent framework modeled on the experience of the ever changing seasonal cycles that rotate through the years and/or the cycles of human existence that go through irreversible stages for each individual yet follow repetitive stages for each succeeding generation. At the same time, intergenerational contact constantly regenerates culture and provides a process of self renewal for a changing people as well as their changing cultures through time.

Ultimately, the ideologically diverse people who make up this world continue to grapple with the interaction of the study of history in the form of the past event, the making of history in the actions of the present and the visions of a better future. As the humanities and social sciences attempt to understand the immediate past history, good theoreticians try to explain those elements in public and private life that cause social change. History as the final product of a searching process of reconstructing history in the hands of scholars is nevertheless an important instructor to future generations. It is this "reconstructed" history that is called upon to "teach the lessons of history." It is also about the creation and articulation of this history that Marcus Garvey's warning is so apt--namely, that a "... people without knowledge of its history is like a tree without roots."

The Africa centered perspective provides the type of history for people of African descent that makes sense of what they, rather than somebody else, went through first. African people still have to learn the history of other peoples in order to become informed citizens of culturally diverse societies of which they are members and the diversity in the world in which they live. However, in order to participate with others without losing their own special identity, special meaning and social bearings, they have to know as a basic foundation of their social knowledge, a focused history of themselves that makes sense. That history of themselves must be one that employs an Africa centered perspective.

The perspective may also allow them to do something more. By separating the broad issues from less ephemeral issues of the time, the Africa centered scholar, may for example, view with the historian-journalist, John Henry Clarke, the long history of African people since 5000 B.C.E. As a futurologist she or he can speculate and gaze beyond the next century.

The long view of time that employs an Africa centered perspective may change the understanding of context and the significance of events that bear on African people and the world. The perspective helps to create in sharp contrast a time map on which to trace the events of the past, create history through action in the present and plot the path of possible future action. It allows one to look at these large chunks of time and to hypothesize and speculate about four historical periods in which Africans excelled beginning with (1) the first period in the fourth millennium B.C.E in Kemet that followed the creation of human cultures and enduring human institutions, (2) the second period between 600 to 1600 in West Africa that witnessed the concentration of state power and the formation of gigantic states, (3) the third period from 1800 to 1890 that saw the attempt to rebuild defensive redoubts through the unification of existing societies throughout the African World and, (4) the fourth emergence in the post-1960 period represented by the Civil Rights Movement in the United States and the struggle for political independence in Africa and the Caribbean during which the African diaspora in the West emerged as a coequal member in the affairs of the African world.

This multi-faceted emergence of the African in politics, culture, arts and literature will probably reach its crest in the twenty first century. Hopefully by then the peoples of the world will have built a consensus that will allow [1] the creation of multiculturally sensitive human sciences and [2] economic development that is both ecologically responsible and socially just. There are serious obstacles in the way. Social disorganization, exploitation and economic poverty, the prevalence of preventible disease, misuse of scarce resources, and instances of short-sighted leadership without vision inside and outside African communities can create major roadblocks.[40]

This tentative but broad historical view of African the possibilities would place the history of the civil rights movement in the United States, the independence movement in Africa and the liberation movement of Southern Africa in an international context of forward motion of Africans in the world. For this reason, Carter G. Woodson, W. B. Rubusana, W.E.B. Du Bois, John de Graft Johnson and Jacob Egharevba represent examples of pioneer retrievers of an Africa centered perspective in history in this century who continued to be hampered by Eurocentric limitations.

However, we should always be aware that the first Africa centered histories were written 4,000 years ago by the contemporaries of Imhotep; or sung by the royal griots of sixteenth-century Mali when they recalled the feats of Sundiata and, in recent times retold through poetry by the Imibongi of Dalindyebo in the nineteenth century. In other words, in the beginning, Africans employed a perspective centered on themselves. Today in order to <u>restore</u> a meaningful perspective and to provide proper insights in the study of African peoples the world over, scholars who study the experience of Africans in African and outside Africa have to examine closely the insights provided by an Africa centered perspective.[41]

There are scholars who are intellectually "uncomfortable" with an Africa centered perspective because they will see it as a return to hegemonic ethnocentricism that characterized the Europe centered knowledge. This is to especially when the term "Afrocentric" is used to describe this new theoretical process of restructuring social knowledge. This negative reaction to the term is tied to the historical experience with a hegemonic Europe centered perspective that was wedded to European imperialism. The term "Africa centered" in this publication refers primarily to the <u>centering</u> of a framework of inquiry and is in no way associated with the <u>denial</u> of the validity of other perspectives. A scholar who writes with a Asia centered perspective is not antithetical to an Africa centered perspective, she or he enriches our understanding of the world by complementing other perspectives. Only a hegemonic perspective falsifies the meaning of words like "universal" and "international." Contemporary international law for example in reality reflects the "European law of Nations" that was extended to the rest of the world in the last four hundred years with the expansion of European colonization and imperialism. It cannot be represented as a system of law that the world's people decided upon voluntarily until the ongoing debates and revisions in United

Nations' sponsored international conferences have so modified its provisions as to make it a reflection of a global consensus.

The Africa centered perspective helps us to re-evaluate words, concepts, and phrases that are usually bandied about without an appreciation of their historical roots and their association to unequal global power alignments.

Ultimately the Africa centered perspective in history should open, in the study of history what theorists of Afrocentricity have already embarked upon in other areas of the human sciences, namely to re-start an intellectual discourse in the continuing struggle to free the minds of men and women from conceptual chains that tie them to unwitting subservience and unconscious bias. Multicentered knowledge systems have to be created to replace the unicentric systems of the present.

The human sciences of the twenty first century will need grounding in the social reality of perceptions and experiences of all peoples on this planet in order to counterbalance the potentially destructive effects of the life threatening military technology that is piling up in the arsenals of the technologically advanced countries. Scholars dedicated to human survival can save future generations from grief by teaching the youth of the last decade of the twentieth century to appreciate the widespread talent, cultural innovativeness and rich intellectual diversity that exists among the people who inhabit this planet.

The application of an Africa centered perspective of history in research will only be one way that will help to bring about the appreciation and understanding of this diversity of the human experience. From such unambiguously centered pools of historical information, better informed and less arrogant human scientists of the twenty first century will embark in a realistic and academically honest refurbishing and re-organization of the 'disciplines' in the human sciences. The concepts that will emerge will be ones that can apply comfortably in a "pluriversal," multicentered and "multicultural" setting. Such concepts will continue to be applicable even when the concepts are shifted from one region of the world to another. The multiple perspectives will have forced a process of winnowing "unicentric" and sexist assumptions from the concepts such as "minority" used in history and the social sciences. The eliminations of such terms alone will be a major step in the process of intellectual liberation of knowledge systems.

An Africa centered perspective of history can be taught and can be learned by any serious student of history. The perspective can also be incorporated into the research design of any scholar who attempts to understand African people how this can be done in their own 'historical terms'. I have tried to describe how this can be done in this brief essay. The details of working out the specific ways in which an Africa centered perspective will affect particular ideologies, methodologies, approaches and research designs will be the concern of future endeavors. If this brief discussion provokes students, historians and human scientists to engage in serious introspection, then I will have accomplished what I set out to do with this essay.

NOTES

[1] The question of perspective raised in this essay should not be confused with the technical concerns of historians who assume that central conceptual issues governing assumptions in African history have been resolved and all that remains is to fine tune methodology, data collection and data analysis. Examples of this focus on the technical mechanics of historical investigation in Africa are to be found in the June 1987 issue of the <u>African Studies Review</u> 30 (June 1987), where articles by Janet Ewald, Thomas Spear, Robert Harms, and Kings M. Phiri demonstrate the major strengths and weaknesses of technical history with ostensibly "universal" or "cosmopolitan" assumptions.

[2] Conal Furay and Michael J. Salevouris, <u>History: A Workbook of Skill Development</u> (New York and London: New Viewpoints, 1979), pp. 1-3. Harry Elmer Barnes, <u>A History of Historical Writing</u>, 2nd. rev. ed. (New York: Dover Publications, 1963), p. 3.

[3] For the insignificant part accorded to African historical experience, see Ernst Breisach's Historiography: Ancient, Medieval and Modern (Chicago and London: University of Chicago Press, 1983) especially chapters 1, 21 and 28. However, the most instructive example of Africa's perceived insignificant role in history is demonstrated by its treatment in the International Handbook of Historical Studies: Contemporary Research and Theory edited by Georg G. Iggers and Harold T. Parker (Westport, Conn.: Greenwood Press, 1979). The book has 21 chapters and is 431 pages long. "Sub-Saharan Africa" is discussed dead last and receives a total complement of 16 pages.

Also see Barnes, History, pp. 307, 310-329 and Joseph L. Esposito, The Transcendence of History: Essays on the Evolution of Historical Consciousness (Athens, Ohio: Ohio University Press, 1984), pp. 49-55, 88-99 and the discussion by Victorino Tejera in History as a Human Science: The Conception of History in Some Classic American Philosophers (Lanham, MD: University Press of America, 1984), pp.15-19, 123-137.

[4] Molefi Kete Asante, Kemet, Afrocentricity and Knowledge (Trenton: Africa World Press, 1990), p. vi.

[5] Asante in The Afrocentric Idea; Wade W. Nobles in "African Philosophy: Foundations for Black Psychology," in Reginald L. Jones, Black Psychology (New York: Harper and Row, 1980), pp. 23-36; Na'im Akbar in Chains of Psychological Slavery (Jersey City, N.J.: New Mind Production, 1984); Maulana Karenga in "Corrective History: Reconstructing the Black Past," First World, 1 (May/June, 1977): 50-54 and Kawaida Theory: An Introductory Outline (Inglewood, Ca.: Kawaida Publications, 1980), pp. 17-18, 21-28, 29-36; Dona Marimba Richards in "The Demystification of Objectivity," Imhotep: An Afrocentric Review 1 (January 1989): 23-34; Ngugi Wa Thiongo, .

[6] James Turner and W. Eric Perkins, " Towards a Critique of Social Science," Black Scholar 7 (April 1976): 2-11; John Horace Parry, Europe and the Wider World, 1415-1715, 3rd rev. (London: Hutchinson, 1966). Jim Haskins and Hugh F. Butts, The Psychology of Black Language (New York: Barnes and Noble Books,

1973), pp. 1-14, 16-18, 28-37, 39-44.

[7] Blaise Diagne is quoted in Rayford W. Logan, "The Historical Aspects of Pan Africanism: A Personal Chronicle," African Forum 1 (Summer, 1965): 95. W.E.B Du Bois in The Souls of Black Folk (Chicago: A. C. McClurg and Company, 1903), pp. 16-17.

[8] Samuel P. Huntington, "The Clash of Civilizations?" Foreign Affairs 72 (Summer 1993): 22-49.

[9] Arthur Schlesinger, Jr., "The Humanist Looks at Empirical Social Research," American Sociological Review 27 (December, 1962): 768-771. R. G. Collingwood, The Idea of History (London and New York: Oxford University Press, 1956), pp. 1-2, 6-7, 9-10; John Lukacs, "The Evolving Relationship of History and Sociology," Politics, Culture and Society 1 (Fall, 1987): 86-87.

[10] Edward N. Saveth, "The Conceptualization of American History" in American History and the Social Sciences edited by Edward N. Saveth (New York: Free Press of Glencoe, 1964) pp. 3-6, 9-12. E. J. Hobsbwam, "From Social History to the History of Society" in

Historical Studies Today, ed. Felix Gilbert and Stephen R. Graubard (New York and London: W. W. Norton and Co., 1972), pp. 1-26.

[11] Furay and Salevouris, History, pp. 17-22; Collingwood, Idea of History, pp. 8-9, 292.

[12] Lukacs, "Evolving Relationship of History and Sociology," pp. 86-87 and more fully discussed in his Historical Consciousness or the Remembered Past (New York, Evanston and London: Harper and Row Publishers, 1968), pp. 1-49, 224-251, 273-315.

[13] Maulana Karenga, Introduction to Black Studies, 2nd Edition (Los Angeles: University of Sankore Press, 1993), p. 70.

[14] The World Almanac and Book of Facts 1988 (New York: Pharos Books, 1987), pp. 522.

[15] The terms "minority" and "majority" outside a global context derive their social meaning on the numerical context of the particular regional or national situation. Terms that reflect relative access to power by different social groups and are transnationally mobile, might be more useful for comparative analysis. E[mmanuel] le Roy Ladurie frankly admits his Western

European focus in discussing rural civilization in The Territory of the Historian translated by Ben and Si^an Reynolds (Chicago: University of Chicago Press, 1979), pp. 79-110.

[16] This discussion of the ideas of William Appleman Williams follows the analysis by David W. Noble in The End of American History: Democracy, Capitalism, and the Metaphor of Two Worlds in Anglo-American Writing, 1880-1980 (Minneapolis: University of Minnesota Press, 1985), pp. 139-140 and in William's Empire as a Way of Life: An Essay on the Causes and Character of America's Present Predicament along with a Few Thoughts about an Alternative (New York and Oxford: Oxford University Press, 1980). Similar sentiments are expressed in Esposito, Transcendence, pp. 88, 91-99.

[17] Noble, End of American History, pp. 116, 137, 146.

[18] Harold Cruse, Crisis of the Negro Intellectual (New York: William Morrow and Co., 1967..) and Plural but Equal: Blacks and Minorities in America's Plural Society (New York: William Morrow and Co. Inc., 1987), pp. 33-34, 66-69, 376-391.

[19] Sande Cohen, <u>Historical Culture: On the Recording of an Academic Discipline</u> (Berkeley, Los Angeles and London: University of California Press, 1986), pp. 1-4. For Martin Bernal see his <u>Black Athena: The Afro-Asiatic, vol.1, The Fabrication of Ancient Greece</u> (New Brunswick, N.J.: Rutgers University Press, 1987), pp. 1-73.

[20] See Eleanor Burke Leacock, <u>Myths of Male Dominance: Collected Articles on Women Cross Culturally</u> (New York and London: Monthly Review Press, 1981), Karen Sacks, <u>Sisters and Wives: The Past and Future of Sexual Equality</u> (Urbana: Illinois University Press, 1982), Sally Slocum, "Woman the Gatherer: Male Bias in Anthropology" in Rayna Reiter, ed., <u>Toward an Anthropology of Women</u> (New York and London: Monthly Review Press, 1979) and Colin Turnbull, "Mbuti Womanhood" in Frances Dahlberg, <u>Woman the Gatherer</u> (New Haven and London: Yale University Press, 1981).

[21] Pierre Joulee, <u>The Pillage of the Third World</u>, trans. by Mary Klopper (New York and London: Monthly Review Press, 1968), pp. 2-3; Paul Bairoch, <u>The</u>

Economic Development of the Third World Since 1900, trans. by Lady Cynthia Postan (Berkeley and Los Angeles: University of California Press, 1975), p. 3; J. E. Goldthorpe, The Sociology of the Third World: Disparity and Involvement (New York, London and Cambridge: Cambridge University Press, 1975), p. 1.

[22] Peter Rigby, Persistent Pastoralists: Nomadic Societies in Transition (London: Zed Press, 1985 and Atlantic Highlands, N.J.: Biblio Distribution Center, 1985), especially pp. 11-22. See the discussion in J. Khan and J. P. Llobera, eds., The Anthropology of Pre-Capitalist Societies (London: MacMillan, 1981) and in Harold Wolpe, ed., The Articulation of Modes and Production (London: Routledge and Kegan Paul, 1980) and Race, Class and the Apartheid State (London: James Curry and Paris: UNESCO, 1988).

[23] See Arnold Temu and Bonaventure Swai's Historians and Africanist History: A Critique (London: Zed Press, 1981) and Maurice Bloch, Marxism and Anthropology: The History of a Relationship (New York and Oxford: Oxford University Press, 1983), pp. 32-43, 140-172.

[25] See Vincent Harding's <u>There is a River: The Black Struggle for Freedom in America</u> (New York: Harcourt, Brace, Jovanovich, 1981); Eugene D. Genovese, <u>From Rebellion to Revolution: Afro-American Slave Revolts in the Making of the Modern World</u> (Baton Rouge and London: Louisiana State University Press, 1979), pp. 1-4, 6-15, 51-75, 126-127. Stephan Thernstrom uses the phrase 'enslaved African' in his contribution on "Ethnic Groups in American History" in Lance Lebman, ed., <u>Ethnic Relations in America: Immigration, The Cities, Lingualism, Ethnic Politics, Group Rights, The American Assembly</u> (Englewood Cliffs, N.J.: Prentice-Hall, 1982), p. 5.

[26] The sixth edition of John Hope Franklin and Alfred A. Moss' otherwise excellent textbook on African American History <u>From Slavery to Freedom: A History of Negro Americans</u> (New York: Alfred A. Knopf, 1988) provides two informative chapters on the African historical background and cultural institutions. However, the title conveys the historical disconnectedness that I indicate here. The use of 'Africans', 'Blacks' and

'Negroes' interchangeably to describe the Africans in colonial America further confuses the definitional issues that I try to unravel here.

A more consistent historical treatment of the Africans in 'colonial and post colonial America is Robert L. Harris Jr.'s publication for the American Historical Association's Teaching Division <u>Teaching Afro-American History</u> (Washington, D.C.: A.H.A.,1985) especially pp. 3-15. However I would substitute my terminology of "free and enslaved Africans and African Americans" for Dr. Harris' "free Africans and slaves. John Blassingame's revised <u>Slave Community: Plantation Life in the Antebellum South</u> (New York: Oxford University Press, 1979) contains an excellent narrative that describes the unfolding social transition from African to African American although the conceptualization of the title would be more consistent as with an Africa centered perspective as <u>The Enslaved African American Community</u>. Vincent Bakpetu Thompson offers a an interesting Africa centered conceptualization in <u>The Making of the African Diaspora in the Americas 1441-1900</u> (New York and London: Longman Inc., 1987).

On the role of the First Americans see James Axtell's The Invasion Within: The Contest of Cultures in Colonial North America (New York and Oxford: Oxford University Press, 1985), esp. pp. 3-19, 242-267 and his The European and the Indian: Essays in the Ethnohistory of Colonial North America (New York and Oxford: Oxford University Press, 1981), pp. 131-167. Other works on First Americans include John R. Alden, John Stuart and the Southern Colonial Frontier: A Study of Indian Relations, War, Trade, and Land Problems in the Southern Wilderness, 1754-1775 (Ann Arbor, Mich.: University of Michigan Press, 1944); Nicholas B. Wainwright, George Croghan: Wilderness Diplomat (Chapel Hill, N.C.: University of North Carolina Press, 1959) and Robert F. Berkhofer, Jr., "Cultural Pluralism versus Ethnocentricism in the New Indian History" in The American Indian and the Problem of History, ed. Calvin Martin (New York and Oxford: Oxford University Press, 1987), pp. 35-45.

[27] See editorial by Mortimer B. Zuckerman titled "The Black Underclass" in U.S. News and World Report (April 14, 1986): 78.

[28] Harris, <u>Afro-American History</u>, pp. 4-10; Nash, <u>Red, White and Black</u>, pp. 298-319.

[29] Peter H. Wood, <u>Black Majority: Negroes in Colonial South Carolina from 1670 through the Stono Rebellion</u> (New York: Alfred A. Knopf, 1974), pp. 271-326.

[30] Thompson, <u>African Diaspora</u>, pp. 62-98, 135-153, Nash, <u>Red, White and Black</u>, pp. 156-212 and Wesley Frank Craven's discussion in <u>White, Red and Black: The Seventeenth Century Virginian</u> (Charlottesville: University of Virginia Press, 1971).

[31] The "contributionist" or vindicationist approach emerged at a time when African Americans were depicted in academic and lay writing as "inferior" intellectually, socially, spiritually, politically and culturally. A great deal of the writing efforts of scholars like W.E.B. Du Bois, Rayford W. Logan and Carter G. Woodson was directed towards refuting this `mainstream' assertion. In less skilled hands, this focus led to narratives that ignored many significant and positive internal developments within the African American community itself--and so encouraged a scholarship

that emphasized how well African Americans performed in specific fields compared to ambiguously defined "mainstream" members. In the process, this particular focus peripheralized what was going on in the African American community until a "social crisis" of one kind or another in the African American community became highly publicized in the "mainstream" media.

[32] See M. Whiting Spilhaus, <u>South Africa in the Making 1652-1806</u> (Cape Town: Juta and Co., 1966) and Leo Fouche, "The Foundation of the Cape Colony 1652-1708" in <u>The Cambridge History of the British Empire vol. 8 South Africa</u>. M. F. Katzen writing in the <u>Oxford History of South Africa vol.1. South Africa to 1870</u>, eds. Monica Wilson and Leonard Thompson (New York and Oxford: Oxford University Press, 1969) calls his chapter "White Settlers and the Origin of a New Society 1652-1778." Richard Elphick and Hermann Giliomee edited a book titled <u>The Shaping of South African Society 1652-1820</u> (Cape Town and London: Longman Penguin Southern Africa, 1979).

Radical writing includes Helen Bradford's "Class Contradictions and Class Alliances: The Social Nature of ICU Leadership, 1924-1929," in Resistance and Ideology in Settler Societies, Southern Africa Studies vol. 4, ed. Tom Lodge (Johannesburg: Ravan Press, 1987) and Saul Dubow's "Race, Civilization and Culture: The Elaboration of Segregationist Discourse in the Interwar Years" in Shula Marks and Stanley Trapido eds. The Politics of Race, Class and Nationalism in Twentieth Century South Africa (London and New York: Longman Inc., 1987).

[33] See the discussion in Maria Van Diepen, ed., The National Question in South Africa (London and Atlantic Highlands, N.J.: Zed Books, 1988); Neville Alexander, Sow the Wind: Contemporary Speeches (Johannesburg: Skotaville Publishers, 1985); Harry Mashabela, A People On the Boil: Reflections on Soweto (Johannesburg: Skotaville Publishers, 1987); Lou Turner and John Alan, Frantz Fanon, Soweto and American Black Thought (Chicago: News and Letters, 1986); Robert Jefferson, Jr., Black Consciousness in South Africa: The Dialectics of Ideological Resistance to White Supremacy (Albany: State University of New York Press, 1986); Gail Gerhart, Black Power in South

Africa (Berkeley: University of California Press, 1978).

[34] See treatment of this topic in the author's "Tsa Batho: The Zonal Dynamics of Black Politics in South Africa," in Edmond J. Kelley and Louis A. Picard, eds., South Africa in Southern Africa: Domestic Change and International Conflict (Boulder, Colo.: Lynne Reinner, 1989) and William Beinart's "Worker Consciousness, Ethnic Participation and Nationalism: The Experience of a South African Migrant, 1930-1960" in Marks and Trapido, Politics of Race, pp. 286-309.

[35] An illuminating discussion of the Toi-toi is to be found in Alven Makapela's paper "The Toi in Historical Perspective" read at the Annual Conference of the Association for the Study of Afro-American Life and History, October 7, 1988, Cherry Hill, New Jersey.

[36] T. R. Davenport, South Africa: A Modern History, 3rd ed. (Toronto and Buffalo: University of Toronto, 1987), pp. 1-252.

[37] Wolpe, Race and Class, pp. 48-59. Bill Freund, The Making of Contemporary Africa: The Development of African Society Since 1800 (Bloomington: Indiana University Press, 1984), pp. 1-15. John Iliffe, The

Emergence of African Capitalism (Minneapolis: University of Minnesota Press, 1983), pp. 1-43. See the central issues raised by Craig Calhoun in The Question of Class Struggle: Social Foundations of Popular Radicalism During the Industrial Revolution (Chicago and Oxford: University of Chicago Press, 1982), pp. vii-xiv, 3-33.

[38] Cheikh Anta Diop, The African Origins of Civilization: Myth or Reality, ed. and trans. Mercer Cook (Westport, Conn.: Lawrence Hill and Co., 1974), p. xiv.

[39] Carter G. Woodson, The Miseducation of the Negro (Washington, D.C.: Associated Publishers, Inc., c. 1933).

[40] See St. Clair Drake, Black Folk Here and There: An Essay in History and Anthropology Vol. 1 (Los Angeles: Center for Afro-American Studies, 1987). Yosef A. A. Ben-Jochannan, Africa: Mother of Western Civilization (New York: Alkebu-lan Books Associates, 1971). John C. De Graft-Johnson, African Glory: The Story of Vanished Negro Civilizations (New York: Walker and Co., 1966). E. Jefferson Murphy, History of African

Civilization (New York: Dell Publishing Co., 1972).

[41] See Joseph C. Miller, ed., The African Past Speaks: Essays on Oral Tradition and History (Hampden, Conn.: Shoe String Press and Co., 1980); E. J. Alagoa and K. Williamson, Ancestral Voices: Historical Texts From Nembe, Niger Delta, Jos Oral History and Literature Texts, (Jos: University of Jos, 1983); T. Cope, ed., Izibongo: Zulu Praise Poems (Oxford: Clarendon Press, 1968); Ruth Finnegan, Oral Literature Africa (Nairobi: Oxford University Press, 1970); Djibril Tamsir Niane, Soundjata on L'Epopee Mandingue (Paris: Presence Africaine, 1960); Jan Vansina, Oral Tradition as History (Madison: University of Wisconsin Press, 1985).

GLOSSARY

Certain words and phrases are given special meaning in this publication as part of the ongoing effort to clarify Africa centered scholarship. I have also accepted the current conventional meaning given to certain terms although I would like to see them change in the future. There are no "non-people" in the text because of my firm believe that every people on this earth is a positive presence and cannot therefore be defined in the negative even when they have a record of doing negative things to other human beings.

Africans:

People who were born in Africa. Their principal identity does not change whether they are taken to the Asian, European or American continent. Some descendants of Africans chose to retain the name African in describing themselves.

African Americans:

The group of people in America [creole population

after the first generation of Africans] who trace their ancestry to the African continent regardless of region. This group has usually been referred to as Blacks, Negroes, negroes, Coloreds or as Afro-Americans, Black Americans, Negro Americans and Colored Americans. One should watch the use of the term Black or Colored when it applies to people of African, Asian, and American origin or peoples from all over the world who have intermixed 'racially'. In the latter case the terms are not equivalent with African American.

Afrikaners:

The immigrant population of Dutch, French and German descent who had arrived in South Africa by 1700 have appropriated this title for themselves in the official literature of their minority government. Indigenous Africans seem to have a hard time in official literature claiming what they certainly consider their identity--namely, African. They have been historically considered 'Blacks', 'Bantu', 'Natives', etc.

Blacks:

This term as it is used in the South African context refers to South Africans excluding European South

Africans and covers the majority indigenous Africans, those of Asian descent and those of mixed African, Asian or/and European descent also known as "Coloureds." The term replaces the unlikely "Non-European and Non-White that still clutter literature on about South Africa.

In the context of the United States, Black is usually an equivalent of African American, Negro and Colored.

Enslaved:

This adjective is used to describe the African or second generation African Americans who were kept in a condition of servitude against their will. I find it to be more accurate than the simple us of the term slave which permanently defines a people in terms of their temporary social condition and has led to the anomaly of referring to the culture that enslaved African Americans created as "slave culture.

European Americans:

The majority and dominant group in the history and politics of the United States of America that is usually called white Americans or simply Americans without qualification. The use of the term American in this publication refers to all peoples of the United States. A great deal of confusion for the other groups of Americans can be avoided if we consider all Americans as historically "hyphenated Americans" because Americans [with the exception of the First Americans], arrived from other shores since 1500. In this publication I have used the "parochial" definition of American that excludes the Americans from other parts of North and South America. A better term is needed to distinguish between the "parochial" and the "broad" definition of American.

First Americans:

The aboriginal group of Americans that is usually called Native Americans or American Indians. America as used in this publication refers to the United States of America. A continental definition will change the meaning and connotations of the terms attached to the word 'America'. This needs to be done for consistency and accuracy. I have not explored this development which requires a multilingual perspective.

Polycentric:

Analysis that is cognizant of multiple perspectives to the study of social phenomena. A scholar may justify the efficacy of one perspective for a given topical area but this is done to elucidate what other perspectives have been blind to. This assumes a nonhegemonic approach and is not associated with imperial connections of knowledge formation.

Trade in Enslaved Africans:

What is usually referred to as the African Slave Trade in most book. Since Africans did not control this trade, although some Africans participated in it, the phrase 'African slave trade' is confusing and misleading. This was a European Trade in Enslaved Africans to distinguish it from the Asian Trade in Enslaved Africans. One could decide to use the religious identity of those who controlled this trade. In that case I would have to be consistent and discuss the Christian Trade in Enslaved Africans in the west and the Muslim Trade in Enslaved Africans in the north and the east.

Unicentric:

Analysis of social phenomena that uses a single "center." Terms like "Near East" are examples of unicentric conceptualization and when they are imposed on the global grids of knowledge, they become hegemonic tools. The conceptualization about the history of Ancient Kemet is currently a contested terrain between "established Egyptologists" who have employed a Eurocentric framework since the early nineteenth century and scholars who employ an Afrocentric framework. This conflict of frameworks, which is unavoidable, is often depicted as a debate about the racial identity of the people of Ancient Kemet [Egypt].

Universal and Pluriversal:

These two terms are used to reflect the difference between an approach that admits of global diversity and treads wearily on making definitions that totalize the human experience by admitting the "pluriversal" and the tendency to totalize from partial experience by claiming the "universal."

SELECT BIBLIOGRAPHY

Asante, Molefi Kete. The Afrocentric Idea. Philadelphia: Temple University Press, 1987.

_____. Afrocentricity. Trenton, N.J.: Africa World Press, 1988.

_____. Kemet, Afrocentricity and Knowledge. Trenton, N.J.: Africa World Press, 1990.

Diop, Cheikh Anta. Civilization or Barbarism: An Authentic Anthropology. Translated from French by Yaa-Lengi Meema Ngemi. Edited by Harold J. Salemson and Marjolin de Jager. New York: Lawrence Hill Books, 1991.

Drake, St. Clair. Black Folk Here and There: An Essay in History and Anthropology. Volume 1. Los Angeles: Center for Afro-American Studies, 1987.

Jean, Clinton M. Behind Eurocentric Veils: The Search for African Realities. Amherst, Mass.: University of Massachusetts Press, 1991.

Karenga, Maulana. Introduction to Black Studies, 2nd Edition. Los Angeles: University of Sankore Press, 1993.

Keto, C. Tsehloane. The Africa Cantered Perspective of History. Blackwood, N.J.: K. A. Publications, 1989.

Levine, Lawrence W. Black Culture and Black Consciousness: Afro-American Folk Thought from Slavery to Freedom. Oxford, London & New York: Oxford University Press, 1977.

Meyers, Linda James. Understanding the Afrocentric Worldview. Dubuque, Iowa: Kendall-Hunt, 1988.

Smith, Ken. The Changing Past: Trends in South African Historical Writing. Athens, Ohio: Ohio University Press, 1989.

Welsh-Asante, Kariamu, ed. *The African Aesthetic: Keeper of the Traditions*. Westport, CT: Greenwood Press, 1993.